Cheesecakes

Anne Ager

Contents

First published in 1981 by Octopus Books Limited
59 Grosvenor Street, London W1

Third impression, 1981

© 1981 Hennerwood Publications Limited

ISBN 0 906320 47 X

Printed in England by Severn Valley Press Limited

INTRODUCTION

The cheesecake started life in Russia and Eastern Europe well over a century ago. These original cheesecakes were based on a stiff, curd-type cheese that was often homemade, and the cheesecakes were baked. Their more modern American-style counterpart, which is based on a soft full fat cheese and set with gelatine, is very popular and well known everywhere. But many countries have their own particular cheesecake recipe or recipes, all varying greatly in texture, taste and appearance.

The cheesecake has gained tremendous popularity in this country during the last ten years or so. There is, however, a certain 'mystique' attached to the making of a cheesecake, similar to that attributed to the soufflé. Many people who have enjoyed a bought cheesecake are reluctant to embark on making one at home, as they feel special skills and techniques are necessary. This is not so. All that is needed are the right ingredients and care in the making.

There are basically two different types of cheesecake: those that are baked and those that are uncooked. Either type can be sweet or savoury, according to the ingredients that are used. In general, a baked cheesecake is made with sieved cottage cheese, curd cheese or Ricotta (the Italian curd cheese), mixed with eggs, cream, a little flour to stabilize the other ingredients, and a flavouring such as fruit rind, fruit purée, cocoa, etc. An uncooked cheesecake is based on full fat soft cheese, with sugar, egg yolks, cream,

dissolved gelatine, flavouring and whisked egg whites folded in. The amount of sugar used may be reduced if you prefer a less sweet result.

Traditionally, a cheesecake has an edible base, which makes serving much easier, as there is something to hold the cheese filling. The type of base used depends on the filling.

For a biscuit base, finely or coarsely crushed biscuits are mixed with melted butter or margarine, pressed evenly on to the bottom of the cake tin and chilled for 20–30 minutes before adding the filling. If the filling is sweet, sugar may be added to the biscuit base, which is usually made from digestive or other sweet crumbly biscuits. For a savoury cheesecake, unsweetened dry biscuits such as water biscuits are used, and grated cheese, herbs, salt and pepper and other savoury ingredients can be added. Some breakfast cereals, mixed with melted butter, sugar, golden syrup or honey, make an excellent base for a sweet cheesecake.

Shortcrust pastry, pâte sucrée (a sweet shortcrust pastry), shortbread and hot water crust pastry are all suitable for a cheesecake base, according to the type of filling. For an uncooked cheesecake, the pastry base is baked in advance.

A sponge base is only suitable for a sweet cheesecake. With a cooked cheesecake, the sponge base can be baked before the filling is added, to prevent the base and cheesecake filling blending together during cooking. Thin layers of sponge for uncooked cheesecake bases can be bought from many good grocers;

alternatively one-third or half quantity of a normal sponge sandwich mixture can be baked in the appropriately sized tin.

The tin or mould used for a cheesecake is just as important as the right ingredients because cheesecakes are served turned out. This requires a loose-bottomed cake tin, of which there are two main types readily available. The round cake tin with a loose base which simply lifts out comes in a variety of sizes, in ordinary metals or with a non-stick finish. (Non-stick tins are particularly suitable for cheesecake-making, as they ensure very smooth sides to the finished cheesecake.) The continental-style springform cake tin has a loose base and a spring clip on the side of the tin. When the spring is released, the sides separate from the base. The only disadvantage with the springform tin is that it is only widely available in quite large sizes, i.e. 25 cm/10 inches upwards. There are some recipes for large cheesecakes in the party chapter of this book.

Storing cheesecakes

Uncooked and cooked cheesecakes can be stored in the refrigerator for up to 4 days, covered lightly with cling wrap. Cooked savoury cheesecakes are best made and served on the same day.

To freeze: Open-freeze a cheesecake on its tin base and wrap in freezer wrap or a large freezer bag. Keeps for up to 6 months. Elaborately-decorated cheesecakes are best frozen without their decoration, the topping can be added once the cheesecake has thawed. Thaw frozen cheesecakes for 4–6 hours.

The secrets of successful cheesecake making

There are only a few points to watch when making a cheesecake, and if you follow these tips carefully you can be assured of success every time.

For cooked cheesecakes:
1 It is advisable to grease tins lightly, unless they have a non-stick finish. Make sure that the chosen cheesecake base completely covers the bottom of the tin; this prevents any filling seeping through, and gives a neater finished result.
2 Cream the cheese, egg yolks and other ingredients thoroughly together to give a really smooth texture. This can be done quite successfully with a wooden spoon, but if you have an electric mixer you will achieve an even better result.
3 Whisk the egg whites until they are stiff enough to hold soft peaks – they should be of the same texture as the cheese mixture.
4 Fold the whisked egg whites in lightly but thoroughly, to avoid bubbles of egg white being left throughout the mixture. Do not beat the egg whites in or you will lose all the air and lightness.
5 Make sure that the cheesecake mixture is level in the tin before putting it into the oven. Either spread lightly with a knife, or tap the tin gently so the mixture will find its own level.
6 Once the cheesecake is cooked, leave it in the oven to cool slowly – turn off the oven, and leave the door ajar. This helps to prevent excess shrinkage of the cheesecake. Do not be worried, however, as all cooked cheesecakes shrink slightly.

For uncooked cheesecakes:
Points 1, 2, 3 and 4 for cooked cheesecakes also apply to uncooked ones.
1 Make sure that the gelatine is completely dissolved before adding it to the cheese mixture.
2 Mix the dissolved gelatine evenly into the cheese mixture, to avoid any 'streaks' of jelly.
3 Once the cheese mixture starts to thicken, fold in the whisked egg whites lightly but thoroughly.
4 To turn out the set cheesecake, wring out a cloth in very hot water and wipe it around the outside of the tin, to loosen the mixture. If the cheesecake is stubborn, dip a thin-bladed knife into hot water and run it around the edge, between the cheesecake and the tin.

The recipes in this book are many and varied, some sweet, some savoury, some specially for parties, and some 'not-quite-cheesecakes'. Although they can be extravagant and rich tasting, savoury cheesecakes make a perfect supper or lunch dish for the family, and a pleasant change from a quiche or pizza.

The metric and imperial measurements have been calculated separately and may vary in individual recipes. Use one set of measurements as they are not exact equivalents.

COOKED SWEET CHEESECAKES

Cooked sweet cheesecakes are reasonably
economical, both on your purse and on your time.
They are based on the cheaper varieties of cheese
– cottage or curd – and take a shorter time to
prepare than many less inspiring desserts.
If you are making a cheesecake with a sponge
base, it may be baked in the oven for 10–15
minutes before the filling is added so that the two
parts remain completely separate during the
following cooking.

Basic cooked cheesecake

Metric	Imperial
75 g butter or margarine	3 oz butter or margarine
50 g caster sugar	2 oz caster sugar
175 g digestive biscuits, finely crushed	6 oz digestive biscuits, finely crushed

Filling:

Metric	Imperial
225 g curd or sieved cottage cheese	8 oz curd or sieved cottage cheese
3 eggs, separated	3 eggs, separated
few drops of vanilla essence	few drops of vanilla essence
100 g caster sugar	4 oz caster sugar
30 g plain flour	1 oz plain flour
150 ml double or whipping cream	¼ pint double or whipping cream
150 ml soured cream	¼ pint soured cream

Preparation time: 40 minutes
Cooking time: 1½–1¾ hours
Oven: 160°C, 325°F, Gas Mark 3

Melt the butter or margarine and sugar in a saucepan over a gentle heat. Stir in the biscuit crumbs. Press evenly over the bottom of a greased loose-bottomed 18–20 cm/7–8 inch round cake tin. Chill while you make the filling.

Soften the cheese in a large mixing bowl. Beat in the egg yolks, vanilla essence, 50 g/2 oz of the caster sugar, the flour and double cream. Whisk the egg whites until stiff, then whisk in the remaining caster sugar. Fold lightly but thoroughly into the cheese mixture. Spoon the mixture into the prepared tin and smooth the surface.

Bake in a preheated oven for 1½–1¾ hours or until firm but still spongy to the touch. Turn off the oven, open the door and leave the cheesecake to cool in the oven for 1 hour.

Spread the soured cream evenly over the top of the cooked cheesecake and chill in the tin for 3–4 hours. Ease the sides of the tin carefully away from the cheesecake and lift the cheesecake out on the tin base. The cheesecake may be decorated with canned or fresh fruit before serving.
Serves 8

Normandy cheesecake

Metric	Imperial
75 g butter or margarine	3 oz butter or margarine
50 g caster sugar	2 oz caster sugar
100 g digestive biscuits, finely crushed	4 oz digestive biscuits, finely crushed
50 g nuts, finely chopped	2 oz nuts, finely chopped

Filling:

Metric	Imperial
225 g curd or sieved cottage cheese	8 oz curd or sieved cottage cheese
3 eggs, separated	3 eggs, separated
100 g caster sugar	4 oz caster sugar
grated rind of ½ lemon	grated rind of ½ lemon
good pinch of ground mixed spice	good pinch of ground mixed spice
30 g plain flour	1 oz plain flour
25 g sultanas	1 oz sultanas
150 ml double or whipping cream	¼ pint double or whipping cream
1 large dessert apple, cored and thinly sliced	1 large dessert apple, cored and thinly sliced
3 × 15 ml spoons apricot jam	3 tablespoons apricot jam
2 × 15 ml spoons water	2 tablespoons water

Preparation time: 55 minutes
Cooking time: 1½–1¾ hours
Oven: 160°C, 325°F, Gas Mark 3

Melt the butter or margarine and sugar in a saucepan over a gentle heat. Stir in the biscuit crumbs and nuts. Press evenly over the bottom of a greased loose-bottomed 18–20 cm/7–8 inch round cake tin. Chill while you make the filling.

Soften the cheese in a large mixing bowl. Beat in the egg yolks, 50 g/2 oz of the caster sugar, the lemon rind, spice, flour, sultanas and cream. Whisk the egg whites until stiff, then whisk in the remaining caster sugar. Fold lightly but thoroughly into the cheese mixture. Spoon the mixture into the prepared tin and smooth the surface. Arrange overlapping slices of apple in concentric circles on top of the filling.

Bake in a preheated oven for 1½–1¾ hours or until firm but still spongy to the touch. Turn off the oven, open the door and leave the cheesecake to cool in the oven for 1 hour.

Put the apricot jam in a saucepan with the water and bring just to the boil. Press the mixture through a sieve, then brush the apricot glaze evenly over the top of the cheesecake. Chill in the tin for 2–3 hours.

Ease the sides of the tin away from the cheesecake and lift the cheesecake out on the tin base.
Serves 8

Basic cooked cheesecake;
Normandy cheesecake

Rhubarb and orange cheesecake

Metric
75 g butter or margarine
50 g caster sugar
175 g digestive biscuits, finely crushed
grated rind of 1 orange
good pinch of ground ginger

Filling:
225 g rhubarb, chopped
juice of 1 orange
175 g caster sugar
225 g curd or sieved cottage cheese
3 eggs, separated
30 g plain flour

Topping:
75 g plain flour
40 g butter
50 g demerara sugar
150 ml double or whipping cream, stiffly whipped
crystallized orange segments

Imperial
3 oz butter or margarine
2 oz caster sugar
6 oz digestive biscuits, finely crushed
grated rind of 1 orange
good pinch of ground ginger

Filling:
8 oz rhubarb, chopped
juice of 1 orange
6 oz caster sugar
8 oz curd or sieved cottage cheese
3 eggs, separated
1 oz plain flour

Topping:
3 oz plain flour
1½ oz butter
2 oz demerara sugar
¼ pint double or whipping cream, stiffly whipped
crystallized orange segments

Preparation time: 1 hour 20 minutes (plus chilling)
Cooking time: 1½–1¾ hours
Oven: 160°C, 325°F, Gas Mark 3

Melt the butter or margarine and sugar in a saucepan over a gentle heat. Stir in the biscuit crumbs, orange rind and ground ginger. Press the mixture evenly over the bottom of a greased loose-bottomed 18–20 cm/7–8 inch round cake tin. Chill while you make the filling. Put the rhubarb into a saucepan with the orange juice and 50 g/2 oz of the caster sugar and cook gently until tender. Allow to cool. Soften the cheese in a large mixing bowl. Beat in the egg yolks, 50 g/2 oz of the remaining caster sugar, the flour and cooked rhubarb. Whisk the egg whites until stiff, then whisk in the remaining caster sugar. Fold lightly but thoroughly into the cheese mixture. Spoon the mixture into the prepared tin and smooth the surface.
For the topping, sift the flour into a bowl and rub in the butter until the texture of coarse breadcrumbs. Stir in the demerara sugar. Sprinkle evenly over the top of the cheesecake and bake in a preheated oven for 1½–1¾ hours or until firm but still spongy to the touch. Turn off the oven, open the door and leave the cheesecake to cool in the oven for 1 hour.
Ease the sides of the tin carefully away from the cheesecake and lift the cheesecake out on the tin base. Pipe whipped cream on top and decorate with a few crystallized orange segments.
Chill for 2–3 hours before serving.
Serves 8

Plum cheesecake

Metric
75 g butter or margarine
50 g soft brown sugar
100 g porridge oats
1 egg yolk

Filling:
10 ripe dessert plums, halved and stoned
225 g curd or sieved cottage cheese
3 eggs, separated
few drops of almond essence
100 g caster sugar
30 g plain flour
150 ml double or whipping cream

Imperial
3 oz butter or margarine
2 oz soft brown sugar
4 oz porridge oats
1 egg yolk

Filling:
10 ripe dessert plums, halved and stoned
8 oz curd or sieved cottage cheese
3 eggs, separated
few drops of almond essence
4 oz caster sugar
1 oz plain flour
¼ pint double or whipping cream

Preparation time: 50 minutes (plus chilling)
Cooking time: 1½–1¾ hours
Oven: 160°C, 325°F, Gas Mark 3

Melt the butter or margarine and brown sugar in a saucepan over a gentle heat. Stir in the oats and egg yolk. Press evenly over the bottom of a greased loose-bottomed 18–20 cm/7–8 inch round cake tin. Chill while you make the filling.
Reserve 6 plum halves for decoration. Arrange the remaining plum halves over the oatmeal base in the tin. Soften the cheese in a large mixing bowl. Beat in the egg yolks, almond essence, 50 g/2 oz of the caster sugar, the flour and cream. Whisk the egg whites until stiff, then whisk in the remaining caster sugar. Fold lightly but thoroughly into the cheese mixture. Spoon the mixture into the tin and smooth the surface.
Bake in a preheated oven for 1½–1¾ hours or until firm but still spongy to the touch. Turn off the oven, open the door and leave the cheesecake to cool in the oven for 1 hour.
Ease the sides of the tin carefully away from the cheesecake and lift the cheesecake out on the tin base. Spread soured cream over the top, and decorate with the reserved plum halves and some toasted almonds. Chill for 2–3 hours before serving.
Serves 8

Gooseberry cheesecake

Metric
50 g butter or margarine,
  softened
50 g caster sugar
60 g self-raising flour, sifted
1 × 2.5 ml spoon baking
  powder
pinch of ground mixed spice
1 egg

Filling:
225 g gooseberries
juice of 1 lemon
2 × 15 ml spoons honey
225 g curd or sieved cottage
  cheese
3 eggs, separated
100 g caster sugar
30 g plain flour

Topping:
10 large ripe dessert
  gooseberries, thinly sliced
3 × 15 ml spoons apricot
  jam
1–2 × 15 ml spoons water

Imperial
2 oz butter or margarine,
  softened
2 oz caster sugar
2 oz self-raising flour, sifted
½ teaspoon baking
  powder
pinch of ground mixed spice
1 egg

Filling:
8 oz gooseberries
juice of 1 lemon
2 tablespoons honey
8 oz curd or sieved cottage
  cheese
3 eggs, separated
4 oz caster sugar
1 oz plain flour

Topping:
10 large ripe dessert
  gooseberries, thinly sliced
3 tablespoons apricot
  jam
1–2 tablespoons water

Rhubarb and orange
cheesecake; Gooseberry
cheesecake; Plum cheesecake

Preparation time: 1¼ hours (plus chilling)
Cooking time: 1½–1¾ hours
Oven: 160°C, 325°F, Gas Mark 3

Put the butter or margarine, caster sugar, flour, baking powder, spice and egg into a mixing bowl and beat for 2–3 minutes or until light and creamy. Spread the sponge mixture evenly over the bottom of a greased loose-bottomed 18–20 cm/7–8 inch round cake tin.

For the filling, put the gooseberries into a saucepan with the lemon juice and honey and cook until the fruit is soft. (If the fruit is too sharp, add a little sugar.) Allow to cool. Soften the cheese in a large mixing bowl. Beat in the egg yolks, 50 g/2 oz of the caster sugar, the flour and cooked gooseberries. Whisk the egg whites until stiff, then whisk in the remaining caster sugar. Fold lightly but thoroughly into the cheese mixture. Spoon into the prepared tin and smooth the surface.

Bake in a preheated oven for 1½–1¾ hours or until firm but still spongy to the touch. Turn off the oven, open the door and leave the cheesecake to cool in the oven for 1 hour.

Ease the sides of the tin carefully away from the cheesecake and lift the cheesecake out on the tin base. Arrange the dessert gooseberries, overlapping, on top of the cheesecake. Put the apricot jam into a saucepan with the water and heat until melted, then sieve. Brush the apricot glaze evenly over the sliced gooseberries. Chill for 2–3 hours before serving.
Serves 8

Date and honey cheesecake

Metric
50 g butter or margarine
3 × 15 ml spoons golden
  syrup
175 g rolled oats
1 egg yolk

Filling:
225 g full fat soft cheese
3 eggs, separated
4 × 15 ml spoons thick
  honey
30 g plain flour
4 × 15 ml spoons double or
  whipping cream
100 g stoned dates, chopped
50 g caster sugar

Topping:
3 × 15 ml spoons thick
  honey
100 g stoned dates, chopped
50 g walnuts, coarsely
  chopped

Imperial
2 oz butter or margarine
3 tablespoons golden
  syrup
6 oz rolled oats
1 egg yolk

Filling:
8 oz full fat soft cheese
3 eggs, separated
4 tablespoons thick
  honey
1 oz plain flour
4 tablespoons double or
  whipping cream
4 oz stoned dates, chopped
2 oz caster sugar

Topping:
3 tablespoons thick
  honey
4 oz stoned dates, chopped
2 oz walnuts, coarsely
  chopped

Preparation time: 45 minutes (plus chilling)
Cooking time: 1½–1¾ hours
Oven: 160°C, 325°F, Gas Mark 3

For the flapjack base, melt the butter or margarine and golden syrup in a saucepan. Stir in the rolled oats and egg yolk. Press evenly over the bottom of a greased loose-bottomed 18–20 cm/7–8 inch round cake tin. Chill while you make the filling.

Soften the cheese in a large mixing bowl. Beat in the egg yolks, honey, flour and cream. Fold in the chopped dates. Whisk the egg whites until stiff, then whisk in the caster sugar. Fold lightly but thoroughly into the cheese mixture. Spoon the mixture into the prepared tin and smooth the surface. Bake in a preheated oven for 1½–1¾ hours or until firm but still spongy to the touch. Turn off the oven, open the door and leave the cheesecake to cool in the oven for 1 hour. For the topping, melt the honey in a saucepan over a gentle heat. Stir in the dates and nuts, then spread evenly over the top of the cooled cheesecake. Chill in the tin for 2–3 hours.

Ease the sides of the tin carefully away from the cheesecake and lift the cheesecake out on the tin base. Serves 8

Carrot and almond cheesecake

Metric
50 g butter or margarine,
  softened
50 g caster sugar
60 g self-raising flour, sifted
1 × 2.5 ml spoon baking
  powder
1 egg
few drops of almond essence

Filling:
275 g curd or sieved cottage
  cheese
3 eggs, separated
few drops of almond essence
100 g caster sugar
4 × 15 ml spoons ground
  almonds
juice of 1 orange
2 medium carrots, peeled
  and grated
150 ml double or whipping
  cream

Topping:
150 ml soured cream
2 × 15 ml spoons
  marmalade
50 g nuts, toasted and
  chopped

Imperial
2 oz butter or margarine,
  softened
2 oz caster sugar
2 oz self-raising flour, sifted
½ teaspoon baking
  powder
1 egg
few drops of almond essence

Filling:
10 oz curd or sieved cottage
  cheese
3 eggs, separated
few drops of almond essence
4 oz caster sugar
4 tablespoons ground
  almonds
juice of 1 orange
2 medium carrots, peeled
  and grated
¼ pint double or whipping
  cream

Topping:
¼ pint soured cream
2 tablespoons
  marmalade
2 oz nuts, toasted and
  chopped

Preparation time: 40 minutes (plus chilling)
Cooking time: 1½–1¾ hours
Oven: 160°C, 325°F, Gas Mark 3

Choose young sweet carrots for this cheesecake.

Put the butter or margarine, sugar, flour, baking powder, egg and almond essence into a bowl and beat well for 2–3 minutes or until light and creamy. Spread evenly over the bottom of a greased loose-bottomed 18–20 cm/7–8 inch round cake tin.

To make the filling, soften the cheese in a large mixing bowl. Beat in the egg yolks, almond essence, 50 g/2 oz of the caster sugar, the ground almonds, orange juice, grated carrots and cream. Whisk the egg whites until stiff, then whisk in the remaining caster sugar. Fold lightly but thoroughly into the cheese mixture. Spoon the mixture into the prepared tin and smooth the surface.

Bake in a preheated oven for 1½–1¾ hours or until firm but still spongy to the touch. Turn off the oven, open the door and leave the cheesecake to cool in the oven for 1 hour.

Ease the sides of the tin carefully away from the cheesecake and lift the cheesecake out on the tin base. For the topping, mix the soured cream with the marmalade and spread evenly over the top of the cheesecake. Sprinkle with the nuts. Chill for 2–3 hours. Serves 8

Date and honey cheesecake;
Carrot and almond cheesecake

Cinnamon cherry cheesecake

Metric	Imperial
100 g plain flour	4 oz plain flour
25 g icing sugar	1 oz icing sugar
75 g butter or margarine, softened	3 oz butter or margarine, softened
1 egg yolk	1 egg yolk

Filling:

1 × 425 g can sour cherries, drained	15 oz can sour cherries, drained
225 g curd or sieved cottage cheese	8 oz curd or sieved cottage cheese
3 eggs, separated	3 eggs, separated
1 × 2.5 ml spoon ground cinnamon	½ teaspoon ground cinnamon
100 g caster sugar	4 oz caster sugar
30 g plain flour	1 oz plain flour
150 ml double or whipping cream	¼ pint double or whipping cream

Topping:

150 ml double or whipping cream, stiffly whipped	¼ pint double or whipping cream, stiffly whipped
angelica leaves	angelica leaves
ground cinnamon	ground cinnamon

Preparation time: 45 minutes (plus chilling)
Cooking time: 1½–1¾ hours
Oven: 160°C, 325°F, Gas Mark 3

Sift the flour and icing sugar into a bowl. Add the butter or margarine and egg yolk and work to a smooth soft dough. Roll into a ball and press evenly over the bottom of a greased loose-bottomed 18–20 cm/7–8 inch round cake tin. Chill while you make the filling.

Arrange the cherries over the pastry base. Soften the cheese in a large mixing bowl. Beat in the egg yolks, cinnamon, 50 g/2 oz of the caster sugar, the flour and cream. Whisk the egg whites until stiff, then whisk in the remaining caster sugar. Fold lightly but thoroughly into the cheese mixture. Spoon the mixture into the prepared tin and smooth the surface.

Bake in a preheated oven for 1½–1¾ hours or until firm but still spongy to the touch. Turn off the oven, open the door and leave the cheesecake to cool in the oven for 1 hour.

Ease the sides of the tin carefully away from the cheesecake and lift the cheesecake out on the tin base. Pipe the cream on top of the cheesecake. Decorate with angelica leaves and sprinkle with a little cinnamon. Chill for 2–3 hours before serving.
Serves 8

Blackcurrant cheesecake

Metric	Imperial
50 g butter or margarine	2 oz butter or margarine
50 g caster sugar	2 oz caster sugar
100 g macaroons, finely crushed	4 oz macaroons, finely crushed

Filling:

225 g curd or sieved cottage cheese	8 oz curd or sieved cottage cheese
3 eggs, separated	3 eggs, separated
2 × 15 ml spoons rum	2 tablespoons rum
grated rind and juice of ½ lemon	grated rind and juice of ½ lemon
175 g blackcurrant jam	6 oz blackcurrant jam
30 g plain flour	1 oz plain flour
50 g caster sugar	2 oz caster sugar

Topping:

150 ml double or whipping cream, stiffly whipped	¼ pint double or whipping cream, stiffly whipped
1 × 275 g can blackcurrant pie filling	1 × 10 oz can blackcurrant pie filling

Preparation time: 50 minutes (plus chilling)
Cooking time: 1½–1¾ hours
Oven: 160°C, 325°F, Gas Mark 3

Melt the butter or margarine and sugar in a saucepan over a gentle heat and stir in the macaroon crumbs. Press evenly over the bottom of a greased loose-bottomed 18–20 cm/7–8 inch round cake tin. Chill while you make the filling.

Soften the cheese in a large mixing bowl. Beat in the egg yolks, rum, lemon rind and juice, jam and flour. Whisk the egg whites until stiff, then whisk in the caster sugar. Fold lightly but thoroughly into the cheese mixture. Spoon the mixture into the prepared cake tin and smooth the surface.

Bake in a preheated oven for 1½–1¾ hours or until firm but still spongy to the touch. Turn off the oven, open the door and leave the cheesecake to cool in the oven for 1 hour.

Ease the sides of the tin carefully away from the cheesecake and lift the cheesecake out on the tin base. Pipe the cream in a border around the edge of the cheesecake. Fill the centre with the blackcurrent pie filling. Chill for 2–3 hours before serving.
Serves 8

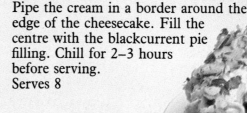

Blackcurrant cheesecake; Cinnamon cherry cheesecake; Prune and cider cheesecake

Prune and cider cheesecake

Metric
75 g butter or margarine
50 g caster sugar
175 g gingernut biscuits,
 finely crushed
grated rind of ½ lemon

Filling:
175 g prunes, soaked
 overnight in 300 ml cider
225 g curd or sieved cottage
 cheese
3 eggs, separated
100 g caster sugar
30 g plain flour
150 ml double or whipping
 cream

Topping:
175 g icing sugar, sifted
grated rind and juice of ½
 lemon
40 g full fat soft cheese

Imperial
3 oz butter or margarine
2 oz caster sugar
6 oz gingernut biscuits,
 finely crushed
grated rind of ½ lemon

Filling:
6 oz prunes, soaked
 overnight in ½ pint cider
8 oz curd or sieved cottage
 cheese
3 eggs, separated
4 oz caster sugar
1 oz plain flour
¼ pint double or whipping
 cream

Topping:
6 oz icing sugar, sifted
grated rind and juice of ½
 lemon
1½ oz full fat soft cheese

Preparation time: 1 hour (plus chilling)
Cooking time: 1½–1¾ hours
Oven: 160°C, 325°F, Gas Mark 3

Melt the butter or margarine and sugar in a saucepan over a gentle heat. Stir in the biscuit crumbs and lemon rind. Press evenly over the bottom of a greased loose-bottomed 18–20 cm/7–8 inch round cake tin. Chill while you make the filling.

Drain off any surplus liquid from the prunes; the liquid can be used to flavour a trifle or other pudding. Stone the prunes. Reserve 6–8 of the prunes for decoration, then arrange the remainder over the biscuit base in the tin.

Soften the cheese in a large mixing bowl. Beat in the egg yolks, 50 g/2 oz of the caster sugar, the flour and cream. Whisk the egg whites until stiff, then whisk in the remaining caster sugar. Fold lightly but thoroughly into the cheese mixture. Spoon the mixture into the prepared tin and smooth the surface.

Bake in a preheated oven for 1½–1¾ hours or until firm but still spongy to the touch. Turn off the oven, open the door and leave the cheesecake to cool in the oven for 1 hour.

Ease the sides of the tin carefully away from the cheesecake and lift the cheesecake out on the tin base. Mix the icing sugar with the lemon rind and juice and sufficient water to give a smooth coating consistency. Spoon over the cheesecake, allowing the icing to trickle down the sides. (The icing can be tinted with a little yellow food colouring, if liked.) Stuff each of the reserved prunes with a little cheese and arrange on top of the cheesecake.

Serves 8

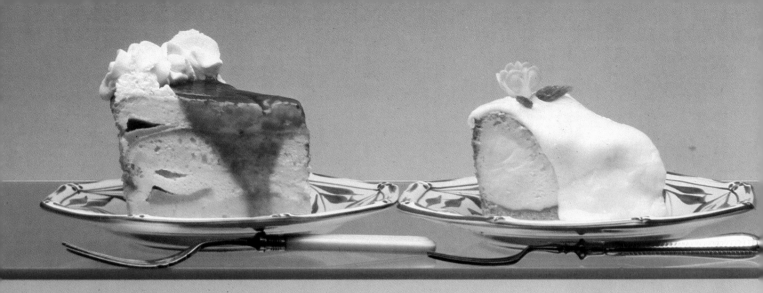

Tipsy cheesecake

Metric	Imperial
1 sponge cake layer, about 2.5 cm deep and 18–20 cm in diameter	1 sponge cake layer, about 1 inch deep and 7–8 inches in diameter
4 × 15 ml spoons sherry	4 tablespoons sherry
225 g full fat soft cheese	8 oz full fat soft cheese
3 eggs, separated	3 eggs, separated
few drops of vanilla essence	few drops of vanilla essence
100 g caster sugar	4 oz caster sugar
30 g plain flour	1 oz plain flour
150 ml whipping cream	¼ pint whipping cream
1 × 425 g can peach slices, drained	1 × 15 oz can peach slices, drained
150 ml double cream, stiffly whipped	¼ pint double cream, stiffly whipped
1 sachet powdered instant jelly glaze	1 sachet powdered instant jelly glaze

Preparation time: 55 minutes (plus chilling)
Cooking time: 1½–1¾ hours
Oven: 160°C, 325°F, Gas Mark 3

Split the sponge cake in half to give two equal layers. Prick all over and moisten with the sherry. Place one layer of sponge in the bottom of a greased loose-bottomed 18–20 cm/7–8 inch round cake tin.

To make the filling, soften the cheese in a large mixing bowl. Beat in the egg yolks, vanilla essence, 50 g/2 oz of the caster sugar, the flour and cream. Whisk the egg whites until stiff, then whisk in the remaining sugar. Fold into the cheese mixture.

Arrange half the canned peach slices on the base sponge layer in the tin. Top with half the filling. Place the second sponge and the remaining peaches on top. Cover with the remaining filling. Bake in a preheated oven for 1½–1¾ hours or until fairly firm. Turn off the oven, open the door and leave the cheesecake there for 1 hour. Ease the sides of the tin away from the cheesecake and lift it out on the tin base. Pipe the cream around the top. Make up the jelly glaze according to the packet instructions. Spoon it over the centre of the cheesecake. Chill for 2–3 hours.
Serves 8

Angel cheesecake

Metric	Imperial
50 g butter or margarine, softened	2 oz butter or margarine, softened
50 g caster sugar	2 oz caster sugar
60 g self-raising flour, sifted	2 oz self-raising flour, sifted
1 × 2.5 ml spoon baking powder	½ teaspoon baking powder
1 egg	1 egg
cochineal	cochineal
275 g full fat soft cheese	10 oz full fat soft cheese
40 g plain flour	1½ oz plain flour
150 ml whipping cream	¼ pint whipping cream
few drops of vanilla essence	few drops of vanilla essence
5 egg whites	5 egg whites
100 g caster sugar	4 oz caster sugar
225 g icing sugar	8 oz icing sugar
1 egg white, lightly whisked	1 egg white, lightly whisked

Preparation time: 45 minutes (plus chilling)
Cooking time: 1½–1¾ hours
Oven: 160°C, 325°F, Gas Mark 3

Put the butter or margarine, sugar, flour, baking powder and egg into a bowl and beat well for 2–3 minutes or until light and creamy. Add a few drops of cochineal to tint the sponge mixture pink. Spread evenly over the bottom of a greased loose-bottomed 18–20 cm/7–8 inch round cake tin.

To make the filling, soften the cheese in a large mixing bowl. Beat in the flour, cream, vanilla essence, one of the egg whites and 50 g/2 oz of the caster sugar. Whisk the remaining egg whites until stiff, then whisk in the remaining caster sugar. Fold lightly but thoroughly into the cheese mixture. Spoon into the tin.

Bake in a preheated oven for 1½–1¾ hours or until firm but still spongy to the touch. Turn off the oven, open the door and leave the cheesecake for 1 hour.

Ease the sides of the tin carefully away from the cheesecake and lift the cheesecake out on the tin base. Sift the icing sugar into a bowl, beat in the egg white and swirl it on top of the cheesecake. Decorate with small sugar flowers, if liked. Chill for 2–3 hours.
Serves 8

Semolina cheesecake

Metric
100 g plain flour
25 g icing sugar
75 g butter or margarine,
  softened
1 egg yolk
225 g curd cheese
grated rind and juice of 2
  lemons
4 × 15 ml spoons semolina
pinch of grated nutmeg
3 eggs, separated
100 g caster sugar
150 ml soured cream
200 ml double or whipping
  cream, stiffly whipped
4 × 15 ml spoons lemon
  curd

Imperial
4 oz plain flour
1 oz icing sugar
3 oz butter or margarine,
  softened
1 egg yolk
8 oz curd cheese
grated rind and juice of 2
  lemons
4 tablespoons semolina
pinch of grated nutmeg
3 eggs, separated
4 oz caster sugar
¼ pint soured cream
⅓ pint double or whipping
  cream, stiffly whipped
4 tablespoons lemon
  curd

Preparation time: 50 minutes (plus chilling)
Cooking time: 1½–1¾ hours
Oven: 160°C, 325°F, Gas Mark 3

Sift the flour and icing sugar into a bowl, add the butter or margarine and egg yolk and work to a soft smooth dough. Roll into a ball and press evenly over the bottom of a greased loose-bottomed 18–20 cm/7–8 inch round cake tin. Chill while you make the filling. Soften the cheese in a large mixing bowl. Beat in the lemon rind and juice, semolina, nutmeg, egg yolks, 50 g/2 oz of the caster sugar and the soured cream. Whisk the egg whites until stiff, then whisk in the remaining caster sugar. Fold lightly but thoroughly into the cheese mixture. Spoon the mixture into the prepared tin and smooth the surface.
Bake in a preheated oven for 1½–1¾ hours or until firm but still spongy to the touch. Turn off the oven, open the door and leave the cheesecake for 1 hour.
Ease the sides of the tin carefully away from the cheesecake and lift the cheesecake out on the tin base. Pipe a lattice of cream on top and fill with lemon curd. Chill for 2–3 hours before serving.
Serves 8

Buttermilk cheesecake

Metric
75 g ground almonds
50 g plain flour, sifted
50 g caster sugar
75 g butter
300 ml buttermilk
225 g full fat soft cheese
3 eggs, separated
few drops of vanilla essence
100 g caster sugar
40 g plain flour
175 g icing sugar
2 × 15 ml spoons clear
  honey
gravy browning

Imperial
3 oz ground almonds
2 oz plain flour, sifted
2 oz caster sugar
3 oz butter
½ pint buttermilk
8 oz full fat soft cheese
3 eggs, separated
few drops of vanilla essence
4 oz caster sugar
1½ oz plain flour
6 oz icing sugar
2 tablespoons clear
  honey
gravy browning

Preparation time: 1 hour 10 minutes (plus chilling)
Cooking time: 1½–1¾ hours
Oven: 160°C, 325°F, Gas Mark 3

Put the almonds, flour, sugar and butter into a bowl and work together to give a smooth paste. Press evenly over the bottom of a greased loose-bottomed 18–20 cm/7–8 inch round cake tin. Chill.
Boil the buttermilk until reduced by half – you should have exactly 150 ml/¼ pint. Allow to cool. Soften the cheese in a large mixing bowl. Beat in the egg yolks, vanilla essence, 50 g/2 oz of the caster sugar, the flour and the cooled buttermilk. Whisk the egg whites until stiff, then whisk in the remaining caster sugar. Fold into the cheese mixture. Spoon into the tin.
Bake in a preheated oven for 1½–1¾ hours or until firm but still spongy to the touch. Turn off the oven, open the door and leave the cheesecake to cool for 1 hour. Ease the sides of the tin carefully away from the cheesecake and lift the cheesecake out on the tin base. Sift the icing sugar into a bowl and beat in the honey and a little water to give a coating consistency. Add a little gravy browning to give a 'butterscotch' colour. Spread the icing evenly over the cheesecake. Chill for 2–3 hours. For a special occasion, pipe on whipped cream and decorate with ice cream wafers.
Serves 8

Coffee cheesecake

Preparation time: 50 minutes (plus chilling)
Cooking time: $1\frac{1}{2}$–$1\frac{3}{4}$ hours
Oven: 160°C, 325°F, Gas Mark 3

Metric
75 g plain flour
50 g icing sugar
50 g butter or margarine,
  softened
50 g nuts, finely chopped
1 egg yolk
1 × 15 ml spoon double
  cream

Imperial
3 oz plain flour
2 oz icing sugar
2 oz butter or margarine,
  softened
2 oz nuts, finely chopped
1 egg yolk
1 tablespoon double
  cream

Filling:
1 × 15 ml spoon instant
  coffee powder (full-
  flavoured variety)
2 × 15 ml spoons boiling
  water
225 g curd or sieved cottage
  cheese
3 eggs, separated
50 g soft brown sugar
30 g plain flour
150 ml hazelnut-flavoured
  yogurt
50 g caster sugar

Filling:
1 tablespoon instant coffee
  powder (full-flavoured
  variety)
2 tablespoons boiling
  water
8 oz curd or sieved cottage
  cheese
3 eggs, separated
2 oz soft brown sugar
1 oz plain flour
$\frac{1}{4}$ pint hazelnut-flavoured
  yogurt
2 oz caster sugar

Topping:
1 × 5 ml spoon instant
  coffee powder
2 × 5 ml spoons boiling
  water
150 ml soured cream
few toasted flaked
  hazelnuts (optional)

Topping:
1 teaspoon instant coffee
  powder
2 teaspoons boiling
  water
$\frac{1}{4}$ pint soured cream
few toasted flaked
  hazelnuts (optional)

Sift the flour and icing sugar into a bowl. Rub in the butter or margarine, then add the chopped nuts and the egg yolk mixed with the cream. Work to a soft smooth dough. Roll into a ball and press evenly over the bottom of a greased loose-bottomed 18–20 cm/7–8 inch round cake tin. Chill while you make the filling. Dissolve the instant coffee in the boiling water. Soften the cheese in a large mixing bowl. Beat in the egg yolks, soft brown sugar, flour, yogurt and the coffee. Whisk the egg whites until stiff, then whisk in the caster sugar until glossy. Fold lightly but thoroughly into the cheese mixture. Spoon the mixture into the prepared tin and smooth the surface.
Bake in a preheated oven for $1\frac{1}{2}$–$1\frac{3}{4}$ hours or until firm but still spongy to the touch. Turn off the oven, open the door and leave the cheesecake to cool in the oven for 1 hour.
For the topping, dissolve the coffee in the boiling water and stir into the soured cream. Spoon evenly over the top of the cooked cheesecake. Sprinkle with a few toasted flaked hazelnuts. Chill for 2–3 hours.
Ease the sides of the tin carefully away from the cheesecake and lift the cheesecake out on the tin base.
Serves 8

Chocolate cheesecake

Metric
75 g butter or margarine
25 g caster sugar
175 g chocolate-coated
  digestive biscuits, finely
  crushed

Filling:
100 g plain chocolate
275 g full fat soft cheese
3 eggs, separated
1 × 5 ml spoon gravy
  browning
50 g soft brown sugar
30 g plain flour
150 ml soured cream
50 g caster sugar

Topping:
225 g granulated sugar
150 ml water
175 g plain chocolate
50 g butter

Imperial
3 oz butter or margarine
1 oz caster sugar
6 oz chocolate-coated
  digestive biscuits, finely
  crushed

Filling:
4 oz plain chocolate
10 oz full fat soft cheese
3 eggs, separated
1 teaspoon gravy
  browning
2 oz soft brown sugar
1 oz plain flour
¼ pint soured cream
2 oz caster sugar

Topping:
8 oz granulated sugar
¼ pint water
6 oz plain chocolate
2 oz butter

Preparation time: 1 hour 20 minutes (plus chilling)
Cooking time: 1½–1¾ hours
Oven: 160°C, 325°F, Gas Mark 3

Melt the butter or margarine and sugar in a saucepan over a gentle heat. Stir in the biscuit crumbs. Press evenly over the bottom of a greased loose-bottomed 18–20 cm/7–8 inch round cake tin. Chill while you make the filling.

Break the chocolate into pieces and put into a heat-proof bowl over a saucepan of hot water. Stir over a gentle heat until the chocolate has melted. Remove from the heat.

Soften the cheese in a large mixing bowl. Beat in the egg yolks, gravy browning, soft brown sugar, flour, soured cream and melted chocolate. Whisk the egg whites until stiff, then whisk in the caster sugar. Fold lightly but thoroughly into the cheese mixture. Spoon the mixture into the tin and smooth the surface.

Bake in a preheated oven for 1½–1¾ hours or until firm but still spongy to the touch. Turn off the oven, open the door and leave the cheesecake to cool in the oven for 1 hour.

To make the topping, put the sugar and water into a saucepan and stir over a gentle heat until the sugar has dissolved. Bring to the boil and boil gently until syrupy. Remove from the heat and add the chocolate broken into small pieces. Beat to melt the chocolate. Add the butter and beat until the frosting is thick, smooth and glossy.

Ease the sides of the tin carefully away from the cheesecake and lift the cheesecake out on the tin base. Swirl the chocolate frosting over the top and sides of the cheesecake. Chill for 2–3 hours before serving.
Serves 8

Coffee cheesecake; Chocolate cheesecake

Bramley cheesecake

Preparation time: 45 minutes (plus chilling)
Cooking time: 1½–1¾ hours
Oven: 160°C, 325°F, Gas Mark 3

Metric
75 g butter or margarine
50 g caster sugar
175 g digestive biscuits,
  finely crushed
pinch of ground mixed spice

Imperial
3 oz butter or margarine
2 oz caster sugar
6 oz digestive biscuits,
  finely crushed
pinch of ground mixed spice

Filling:
225 g curd or sieved cottage
  cheese
3 eggs, separated
1 × 2.5 ml spoon ground
  mixed spice
100 g caster sugar
grated rind and juice of ½
  lemon
1 large cooking apple,
  peeled, cored and grated
40 g plain flour
75 g Cheddar cheese, grated
6 × 15 ml spoons soured
  cream

Filling:
8 oz curd or sieved cottage
  cheese
3 eggs, separated
½ teaspoon ground mixed
  spice
4 oz caster sugar
grated rind and juice of ½
  lemon
1 large cooking apple,
  peeled, cored and grated
1½ oz plain flour
3 oz Cheddar cheese, grated
6 tablespoons soured
  cream

Topping:
300 ml sweetened apple
  purée
150 ml double or whipping
  cream, stiffly whipped
wedges of eating apple

Topping:
½ pint sweetened apple
  purée
¼ pint double or whipping
  cream, stiffly whipped
wedges of eating apple

Melt the butter or margarine and sugar in a saucepan over a gentle heat and stir in the biscuit crumbs and spice. Press evenly over the bottom of a greased loose-bottomed 18–20 cm/7–8 inch round cake tin. Chill while you make the filling.
Soften the cheese in a large mixing bowl. Beat in the egg yolks, spice, 50 g/2 oz of the caster sugar, the lemon rind and juice, grated apple, flour, grated cheese and soured cream. Whisk the egg whites until stiff, then whisk in the remaining caster sugar. Fold lightly but thoroughly into the cheese mixture. Spoon the mixture into the prepared tin and smooth the surface.
Bake in a preheated oven for 1½–1¾ hours or until firm but still spongy to the touch. Turn off the oven, open the door and leave the cheesecake to cool in the oven for 1 hour.
Ease the sides of the tin carefully away from the cheesecake and lift the cheesecake out on the tin base. Spread the apple purée over the top of the cheesecake. Pipe the cream decoratively on top and decorate with wedges of apple. Chill for 2–3 hours before serving.
Serves 8

Russian cheesecake

Preparation time: 45 minutes (plus chilling)
Cooking time: 1½–1¾ hours
Oven: 160°C, 325°F, Gas Mark 3

Metric
100 g plain flour
25 g icing sugar
75 g butter or margarine,
  softened
1 egg yolk

Imperial
4 oz plain flour
1 oz icing sugar
3 oz butter or margarine,
  softened
1 egg yolk

Filling:
225 g curd or sieved cottage
  cheese
grated rind and juice of ½
  lemon
60 g ground almonds
3 eggs, separated
100 g caster sugar
150 ml soured cream
1 egg white

Filling:
8 oz curd or sieved cottage
  cheese
grated rind and juice of ½
  lemon
2 oz ground almonds
3 eggs, separated
4 oz caster sugar
¼ pint soured cream
1 egg white

Topping:
175 g icing sugar, sifted
2 × 15 ml spoons soured
  cream
grated nutmeg

Topping:
6 oz icing sugar, sifted
2 tablespoons soured
  cream
grated nutmeg

Sift the flour and icing sugar into a bowl, add the butter or margarine and egg yolk and work to a soft smooth dough. Roll into a ball and press evenly over the bottom of a greased loose-bottomed 18–20 cm/7–8 inch round cake tin. Chill while you make the filling.
Soften the cheese in a large mixing bowl. Beat in the lemon rind and juice, ground almonds, egg yolks, 50 g/2 oz of the caster sugar and the soured cream. Whisk the egg whites until stiff, then whisk in the remaining caster sugar. Fold lightly but thoroughly into the cheese mixture. Spoon into the tin.
Bake in a preheated oven for 1½–1¾ hours or until firm but still spongy to the touch. Turn off the oven, open the door and leave the cheesecake for 1 hour.
For the topping, beat the icing sugar with the soured cream and add 1–2 × 15 ml spoons/1–2 tablespoons hot water to give a smooth consistency. Ease the sides of the tin carefully away from the cheesecake and lift the cheesecake out on the tin base. Spoon the icing over the top of the cheesecake, allowing it to trickle down the sides. Sprinkle the top with a little grated nutmeg. Chill for 2–3 hours before serving.
Serves 8

coconut cheesecake

Metric
50 g butter or margarine,
  softened
50 g caster sugar
60 g self-raising flour, sifted
1 × 2.5 ml spoon baking
  powder
1 egg
25 g desiccated coconut

Filling:
75 g desiccated coconut
150 ml boiling milk
225 g full fat soft cheese
juice of 1 lime or ½ lemon
3 eggs, separated
100 g caster sugar
30 g plain flour

Topping:
175 g icing sugar
juice of 2 limes or 1 lemon
green food colouring
50 g desiccated coconut,
  toasted
1 lime, thinly sliced

Imperial
2 oz butter or margarine,
  softened
2 oz caster sugar
2 oz self-raising flour, sifted
½ teaspoon baking
  powder
1 egg
1 oz desiccated coconut

Filling:
3 oz desiccated coconut
¼ pint boiling milk
8 oz full fat soft cheese
juice of 1 lime or ½ lemon
3 eggs, separated
4 oz caster sugar
1 oz plain flour

Topping:
6 oz icing sugar
juice of 2 limes or 1 lemon
green food colouring
2 oz desiccated coconut,
  toasted
1 lime, thinly sliced

Preparation time: 45 minutes (plus chilling)
Cooking time: 1½–1¾ hours
Oven: 160°C, 325°F, Gas Mark 3

For the filling, stir the coconut into the boiling milk and leave to stand for 30 minutes.

Meanwhile, make the sponge base: put the butter or margarine, sugar, flour, baking powder, egg and coconut into a bowl and beat well for 2–3 minutes or until creamy and smooth. Spoon the sponge mixture evenly over the bottom of a greased loose-bottomed 18–20 cm/7–8 inch round cake tin.

Soften the cheese in a large mixing bowl. Beat in the lime juice, egg yolks, 50 g/2 oz of the caster sugar and the flour. Strain the liquid from the coconut, pressing the coconut firmly in the sieve to extract the maximum amount of flavour. Add the coconut milk to the cheese mixture. Whisk the egg whites until stiff, then whisk in the remaining caster sugar. Fold lightly but thoroughly into the cheese mixture. Spoon the mixture into the prepared tin and smooth the surface.

Bake in a preheated oven for 1½–1¾ hours or until firm but still spongy to the touch. Turn off the oven, open the door and leave the cheesecake to cool in the oven for 1 hour.

For the topping, sift the icing sugar into a bowl and beat in the lime juice to give a stiffish icing. If the icing is too slack, add a little extra icing sugar. Tint pale green with a little food colouring. Ease the sides of the tin away from the cheesecake and lift the cheesecake out on the tin base. Spread the green icing over the top and sides of the cheesecake. Scatter over the coconut and decorate with slices of lime.

Serves 8

Bramley cheesecake; Russian cheesecake; Coconut cheesecake

Jamaican ginger cheesecake

Metric
75 g butter or margarine
50 g caster sugar
175 g gingernut biscuits,
 finely crushed

Filling:
275 g curd or sieved cottage
 cheese
3 eggs, separated
3 × 15 ml spoons black
 treacle
50 g soft brown sugar
grated rind and juice of ½
 lemon
30 g plain flour
2 × 5 ml spoons ground
 ginger
6 × 15 ml spoons soured
 cream
50 g caster sugar
75 g crystallized ginger,
 chopped

Topping:
3 × 15 ml spoons lime
 marmalade
150 ml double or whipping
 cream, stiffly whipped
50 g crystallized ginger

Imperial
3 oz butter or margarine
2 oz caster sugar
6 oz gingernut biscuits,
 finely crushed

Filling:
10 oz curd or sieved cottage
 cheese
3 eggs, separated
3 tablespoons black
 treacle
2 oz soft brown sugar
grated rind and juice of ½
 lemon
1 oz plain flour
2 teaspoons ground
 ginger
6 tablespoons soured
 cream
2 oz caster sugar
3 oz crystallized ginger,
 chopped

Topping:
3 tablespoons lime
 marmalade
¼ pint double or whipping
 cream, stiffly whipped
2 oz crystallized ginger

Preparation time: 50 minutes (plus chilling)
Cooking time: 1½–1¾ hours
Oven: 160°C, 325°F, Gas Mark 3

Melt the butter or margarine and sugar in a saucepan over a gentle heat and stir in the gingernut biscuit crumbs. Press evenly over the bottom of a greased loose-bottomed 18–20 cm/7–8 inch round cake tin. Chill while you make the filling.
Soften the cheese in a large mixing bowl. Beat in the egg yolks, treacle, soft brown sugar, lemon rind and juice, flour, ground ginger and soured cream. Whisk the egg whites until stiff, then whisk in the caster sugar. Fold lightly but thoroughly into the cheese mixture, together with the chopped crystallized ginger. Spoon the mixture into the prepared tin and smooth the surface.
Bake in a preheated oven for 1½–1¾ hours or until firm but still spongy to the touch. Turn off the oven, open the door and leave the cheesecake to cool in the oven for 1 hour.
Ease the sides of the tin carefully away from the cheesecake and lift the cheesecake out on the tin base. To make the topping, stir the lime marmalade into the cream and spoon over the top of the cheesecake. Decorate with pieces of crystallized ginger. Chill for 2–3 hours before serving.
Serves 8

Marbled cheesecake; Jamaican ginger cheesecake; Plum pudding cheesecake

Marbled cheesecake

Metric	Imperial
75 g plain flour	3 oz plain flour
2 × 15 ml spoons cocoa or drinking chocolate powder	2 tablespoons cocoa or drinking chocolate powder
50 g icing sugar	2 oz icing sugar
50 g butter or margarine, softened	2 oz butter or margarine, softened
1 egg yolk	1 egg yolk

Filling:	Filling:
225 g curd or sieved cottage cheese	8 oz curd or sieved cottage cheese
3 eggs, separated	3 eggs, separated
100 g caster sugar	4 oz caster sugar
150 ml double or whipping cream	¼ pint double or whipping cream
1 × 15 ml spoon plain flour	1 tablespoon plain flour
few drops of vanilla essence	few drops of vanilla essence
1 × 15 ml spoon cocoa powder	1 tablespoon cocoa powder

Topping:	Topping:
175 g icing sugar, sifted	6 oz icing sugar, sifted
50 g plain chocolate	2 oz plain chocolate

Preparation time: 1 hour (plus chilling)
Cooking time: 1½–1¾ hours
Oven: 160°C, 325°F, Gas Mark 3

Sift the flour, cocoa or chocolate powder and icing sugar into a bowl, add the butter or margarine and egg yolk and work to a soft, smooth dough. Roll into a ball and press evenly over the bottom of a greased loose-bottomed 18–20 cm/7–8 inch round cake tin. Chill while you make the filling.

Soften the cheese in a large mixing bowl. Beat in the egg yolks, 50 g/2 oz of the caster sugar and the cream. Divide the mixture into two equal portions. Beat the flour and vanilla essence into one portion and the cocoa into the other. Whisk the egg whites until stiff, then whisk in the remaining caster sugar. Fold half the egg whites into the plain cheesecake mixture and the remainder into the cocoa mixture. Stir the two mixtures lightly together to give a marbled effect, then spoon into the prepared tin and smooth the surface.

Bake in a preheated oven for 1½–1¾ hours or until firm but still spongy to the touch. Turn off the oven, open the door and leave the cheesecake to cool in the oven for 1 hour.

For the topping, mix the icing sugar with 1–2 × 15 ml spoons/1–2 tablespoons hot water to give a smooth consistency. Spoon evenly over the top of the cheesecake. Break the chocolate into small pieces and melt in a heatproof bowl over a pan of hot water. Pipe the chocolate in evenly spaced circles on the icing, then drag at regular intervals with the tip of a knife to give a feathered effect. Chill for 2–3 hours before serving.
Serves 8

Plum pudding cheesecake

Metric	Imperial
50 g butter or margarine	2 oz butter or margarine
50 g soft brown sugar	2 oz soft brown sugar
60 g self-raising flour, sifted	2 oz self-raising flour, sifted
1 × 2.5 ml spoon baking powder	½ teaspoon baking powder
1 egg	1 egg

Filling:	Filling:
275 g full fat soft cheese	10 oz full fat soft cheese
3 eggs, separated	3 eggs, separated
3 × 15 ml spoons brandy	3 tablespoons brandy
50 g soft brown sugar	2 oz soft brown sugar
40 g plain flour	1½ oz plain flour
3 × 15 ml spoons black treacle	3 tablespoons black treacle
1 × 5 ml spoon ground mixed spice	1 teaspoon ground mixed spice
50 g currants	2 oz currants
50 g sultanas	2 oz sultanas
50 g seedless raisins	2 oz seedless raisins
50 g chopped mixed peel	2 oz chopped mixed peel
2 × 15 ml spoons soured cream	2 tablespoons soured cream
50 g caster sugar	2 oz caster sugar

Topping:	Topping:
150 ml soured cream	¼ pint soured cream
2 × 15 ml spoons brandy or rum	2 tablespoons brandy or rum

Preparation time: 40 minutes (plus chilling)
Cooking time: 1½–1¾ hours
Oven: 160°C, 325°F, Gas Mark 3

Put the butter or margarine, brown sugar, flour, baking powder and egg into a bowl and beat well for 2–3 minutes or until light and creamy. Spread evenly over the bottom of a greased loose-bottomed 18–20 cm/7–8 inch round cake tin.

To make the filling, soften the cheese in a large mixing bowl. Beat in the egg yolks, brandy, soft brown sugar, flour, black treacle, spice, dried fruits, peel and soured cream. Whisk the egg whites until stiff, then whisk in the caster sugar. Fold lightly but thoroughly into the cheese mixture. Spoon the mixture into the prepared tin and smooth the surface.

Bake in a preheated oven for 1½–1¾ hours or until firm but still spongy to the touch. Turn off the oven, open the door and leave the cheesecake to cool in the oven for 1 hour.

Ease the sides of the tin away from the cheesecake and lift the cheesecake out on the tin base. Mix the soured cream with the brandy or rum and spoon over the top of the cheesecake. Chill for 2–3 hours before serving. The cheesecake may be decorated in a festive manner, if liked.
Serves 8

Walnut cheesecake

Metric	Imperial
75 g butter or margarine	3 oz butter or margarine
50 g caster sugar	2 oz caster sugar
175 g shortcake biscuits, finely crushed	6 oz shortcake biscuits, finely crushed

Filling:

225 g curd or sieved cottage cheese	8 oz curd or sieved cottage cheese
3 eggs, separated	3 eggs, separated
4 × 15 ml spoons golden syrup	4 tablespoons golden syrup
30 g plain flour	1 oz plain flour
6 × 15 ml spoons double or whipping cream	6 tablespoons double or whipping cream
50 g caster sugar	2 oz caster sugar
75 g walnuts, chopped	3 oz walnuts, chopped

Topping:

16 walnut halves	16 walnut halves
icing sugar	icing sugar

Preparation time: 40 minutes (plus chilling)
Cooking time: 1½–1¾ hours
Oven: 160°C, 325°F, Gas Mark 3

Melt the butter or margarine and sugar in a saucepan over a gentle heat and stir in the biscuit crumbs. Press evenly over the bottom of a greased loose-bottomed 18–20 cm/7–8 inch round cake tin. Chill while you make the filling.

Soften the cheese in a large mixing bowl. Beat in the egg yolks, golden syrup, flour and cream. Whisk the egg whites until stiff, then whisk in the caster sugar. Fold lightly but thoroughly into the cheese mixture, together with the walnuts. Spoon the mixture into the prepared tin and smooth the surface. Arrange the walnut halves on top of the cheesecake mixture.

Bake in a preheated oven for 1½–1¾ hours or until firm but still spongy to the touch. Turn off the oven, open the door and leave the cheesecake to cool in the oven for 1 hour. Chill in the tin for 2–3 hours.

Ease the sides of the tin carefully away from the cheesecake and lift the cheesecake out on the tin base. Dust the surface with sifted icing sugar.

Serves 8

Caramel-topped cheesecake

Metric	Imperial
50 g butter or margarine, softened	2 oz butter or margarine, softened
50 g soft brown sugar	2 oz soft brown sugar
60 g self-raising flour, sifted	2 oz self-raising flour, sifted
1 × 2.5 ml spoon baking powder	½ teaspoon baking powder
1 egg	1 egg

Filling:

225 g full fat soft cheese	8 oz full fat soft cheese
3 eggs, separated	3 eggs, separated
100 g soft brown sugar	4 oz soft brown sugar
4 × 15 ml spoons condensed milk	4 tablespoons condensed milk
30 g plain flour	1 oz plain flour
6 × 15 ml spoons double cream	6 tablespoons double cream

Topping:

175 g lump or granulated sugar	6 oz lump or granulated sugar
4 × 15 ml spoons water	4 tablespoons water
150 ml double cream, stiffly whipped	¼ pint double cream, stiffly whipped

Preparation time: 1 hour 20 minutes (plus chilling)
Cooking time: 1½–1¾ hours
Oven: 160°C, 325°F, Gas Mark 3

Put the butter or margarine, brown sugar, flour, baking powder and egg into a bowl and beat well for 2–3 minutes. Spread in an even layer over the bottom of a greased loose-bottomed 18–20 cm/7–8 inch round cake tin.

To make the filling, soften the cheese in a large mixing bowl. Beat in the egg yolks, soft brown sugar, condensed milk, flour and cream. Whisk the egg whites until stiff and fold lightly but thoroughly into the cheese mixture. Spoon into the tin.

Bake in a preheated oven for 1½–1¾ hours or until firm but still spongy to the touch. Turn off the oven, open the door and leave the cheesecake to cool in the oven for 1 hour. Brush the inside of the tin projecting above the cooked cheesecake with oil.

For the caramel topping, put the lump sugar and water into a heavy-based saucepan. Dissolve over a gentle heat, stirring once or twice. Bring to the boil and boil steadily, without stirring, until the sugar syrup turns to a golden caramel. Remove the pan from the heat. Pour sufficient caramel over the top of the cheesecake to give a thin even coating. Pour the remaining caramel onto a greased baking sheet. Using a sharp knife dipped in boiling water, mark the caramel topping on the cheesecake into 8 sections.

Slide the set caramel from the baking sheet on to a chopping board and crush coarsely with a rolling pin. Ease the sides of the tin away from the cheesecake and lift the cheesecake out on the tin base. Pipe the cream on top and sprinkle with crushed caramel.

Serves 8

Walnut cheesecake; Caramel-topped cheesecake

UNCOOKED SWEET CHEESECAKES

It is the characteristic smooth, mousse-like texture that distinguishes an uncooked sweet cheesecake from any other. All the recipes in this section specify the use of a full fat soft cheese. You can, however, substitute curd or sieved cottage cheese. The texture will be slightly 'rougher', but the finished cheesecake will look just the same and taste not quite as rich.

Basic uncooked cheesecake; Crystallized fruit cheesecake

Basic uncooked cheesecake

Metric
50 g butter or margarine
50 g caster sugar
100 g digestive biscuits,
 finely crushed

Filling:
225 g full fat soft cheese
2 eggs, separated
100 g caster sugar
grated rind of ½ lemon
few drops of vanilla essence
150 ml double or whipping
 cream
15 g powdered gelatine
5 × 15 ml spoons water

To decorate:
whipped cream
canned or fresh fruit

Imperial
2 oz butter or margarine
2 oz caster sugar
4 oz digestive biscuits,
 finely crushed

Filling:
8 oz full fat soft cheese
2 eggs, separated
4 oz caster sugar
grated rind of ½ lemon
few drops of vanilla essence
¼ pint double or whipping
 cream
½ oz powdered gelatine
5 tablespoons water

To decorate:
whipped cream
canned or fresh fruit

Preparation time: 1 hour 10 minutes (plus chilling)

Melt the butter or margarine and sugar in a saucepan over a gentle heat and stir in the biscuit crumbs. Press evenly over the bottom of a greased loose-bottomed 18–20 cm/7–8 inch round cake tin. Chill while you make the filling.

Soften the cheese in a large mixing bowl. Beat in the egg yolks, 50 g/2 oz of the caster sugar, the lemon rind, vanilla essence and cream. Put the gelatine and water into a small heatproof bowl over a saucepan of hot water and stir until the gelatine has dissolved. Beat the gelatine into the cheese mixture. Leave on one side until the mixture is on the point of setting.

Whisk the egg whites until stiff, then whisk in the remaining caster sugar. Fold lightly but thoroughly into the cheese mixture. Spoon the mixture into the prepared tin and shake the tin gently to level the surface. Chill for 3–4 hours or until the filling is set. Carefully release the sides of the tin from the cheesecake and lift the set cheesecake out on the tin base. Decorate with piped whipped cream and canned or fresh fruit of your choice.
Serves 8

Crystallized fruit cheesecake

Metric
1 thin sponge layer, 18–
 20 cm in diameter and
 1 cm thick

Filling:
225 g full fat soft cheese
2 eggs, separated
100 g caster sugar
grated rind and juice of ½
 lemon
few drops of vanilla essence
150 ml double or whipping
 cream
15 g powdered gelatine
5 × 15 ml spoons water
100 g firm marzipan,
 coarsely grated
100 g assorted glacé or
 crystallized fruits,
 chopped

Topping:
3 × 15 ml spoons apricot
 jam
75 g assorted glacé or
 crystallized fruits,
 chopped

Imperial
1 thin sponge layer, 7–8
 inches in diameter and ½
 inch thick

Filling:
8 oz full fat soft cheese
2 eggs, separated
4 oz caster sugar
grated rind and juice of ½
 lemon
few drops of vanilla essence
¼ pint double or whipping
 cream
½ oz powdered gelatine
5 tablespoons water
4 oz firm marzipan,
 coarsely grated
4 oz assorted glacé or
 crystallized fruits,
 chopped

Topping:
3 tablespoons apricot
 jam
3 oz assorted glacé or
 crystallized fruits,
 chopped

Preparation time: 1¼ hours (plus chilling)

Place the sponge layer in a greased loose-bottomed 18–20 cm/7–8 inch round cake tin, trimming the cake if necessary so that it fits in the bottom of the tin exactly. To make the filling, soften the cheese in a large mixing bowl. Beat in the egg yolks, 50 g/2 oz of the caster sugar, the lemon rind and juice, vanilla essence and cream. Put the gelatine and water into a small heatproof bowl over a saucepan of hot water and stir until the gelatine has dissolved. Beat the gelatine into the cheese mixture. Stir in the marzipan. Leave on one side until the mixture is on the point of setting.

Whisk the egg whites until stiff, then whisk in the remaining caster sugar. Fold lightly but thoroughly into the cheese mixture, together with the chopped glacé or crystallized fruits. Spoon the mixture into the prepared tin and shake the tin gently to level the surface. Chill for 1 hour or until the filling is just set. For the topping, mix the apricot jam with the chopped glacé or crystallized fruits and spread evenly over the top of the cheesecake. Put into the freezer and freeze for 1 hour. The cheesecake should still be slightly frozen when served, rather like a sorbet. Carefully release the sides of the tin from the cheesecake and lift the semi-frozen cheesecake out on the tin base. Serve immediately. The cheesecake will cut more easily if the knife is first dipped into hot water.
Serves 8

Meringue cheesecake

Metric	Imperial
50 g butter or margarine	2 oz butter or margarine
50 g caster sugar	2 oz caster sugar
100 g ratafias, finely crushed	4 oz ratafias, finely crushed
3 egg whites	3 egg whites
pinch of cream of tartar	pinch of cream of tartar
175 g caster sugar	6 oz caster sugar
225 g full fat soft cheese	8 oz full fat soft cheese
2 eggs, separated	2 eggs, separated
100 g caster sugar	4 oz caster sugar
1 × 2.5 ml spoon vanilla essence	½ teaspoon vanilla essence
150 ml double or whipping cream	¼ pint double or whipping cream
15 g powdered gelatine	½ oz powdered gelatine
5 × 15 ml spoons water	5 tablespoons water

Preparation time: 2¼ hours (plus chilling)
Cooking time: 1 hour
Oven: 150°C, 300°F, Gas Mark 2

First make the meringue: grease two baking sheets and dust them lightly with flour. Mark a circle 18–20 cm/7–8 inches in diameter on one of the baking sheets. Whisk the egg whites with the cream of tartar until stiff, then whisk in 75 g/3 oz of the caster sugar and continue whisking until stiff again. Fold in the remaining caster sugar. Spoon just under half the meringue into the circle marked on one baking sheet and spread out evenly so that it comes just within the circle. Spread the remaining meringue in an even layer on the other baking sheet. Bake in a preheated oven for 1 hour or until crisp and just lightly coloured.

Meanwhile, melt the butter or margarine and sugar in a saucepan over a gentle heat and stir in the ratafia crumbs. Press evenly over the bottom of a greased loose-bottomed 18–20 cm/7–8 inch round cake tin. Chill while you make the filling.

Soften the cheese in a large mixing bowl. Beat in the egg yolks, 50 g/2 oz of the caster sugar, the vanilla essence and cream. Put the gelatine and water into a small heatproof bowl over a saucepan of hot water and stir until the gelatine has dissolved. Beat the gelatine into the cheese mixture. Leave on one side until the mixture is on the point of setting.

Crush the layer of baked meringue coarsely, leaving the meringue round intact.

Whisk the egg whites until stiff, then whisk in the remaining caster sugar. Fold lightly but thoroughly into the cheese mixture, together with the crushed meringue. Spoon the mixture into the prepared tin and shake the tin gently to level the surface. Place the meringue round on top. Chill for 3–4 hours.

Carefully release the sides of the tin from the cheesecake and lift the cheesecake out on the tin base.
Serves 8

Marshmallow cheesecake

Metric	Imperial
1 thin sponge layer, 18–20 cm in diameter and 1 cm thick	1 thin sponge layer, 8–9 inches in diameter and ½ inch thick

Filling:

Metric	Imperial
175 g marshmallows	6 oz marshmallows
3 × 15 ml spoons milk	3 tablespoons milk
225 g full fat soft cheese	8 oz full fat soft cheese
2 eggs, separated	2 eggs, separated
100 g caster sugar	4 oz caster sugar
6 × 15 ml spoons soured cream	6 tablespoons soured cream
15 g powdered gelatine	½ oz powdered gelatine
5 × 15 ml spoons water	5 tablespoons water

Topping:

Metric	Imperial
150 ml double or whipping cream, whipped	¼ pint double or whipping cream, whipped
75 g marshmallows, halved	3 oz marshmallows, halved
75 g plain chocolate	3 oz plain chocolate

Preparation time: 1 hour 40 minutes (plus chilling)

Place the sponge layer in a greased loose-bottomed 18–20 cm/7–8 inch round cake tin, trimming the cake if necessary so that it fits in the bottom of the tin exactly. To make the filling, chop the marshmallows into pieces with kitchen scissors – this is much easier than using a knife. Put the marshmallows into a saucepan with the milk and stir over a very gentle heat until the marshmallows have melted. Remove from the heat. Soften the cheese in a large mixing bowl. Beat in the egg yolks, 50 g/2 oz of the caster sugar, the melted marshmallows and the soured cream. Put the gelatine and water into a small heatproof bowl over a saucepan of hot water and stir until the gelatine has dissolved. Beat the gelatine into the cheese mixture. Leave on one side until the mixture is on the point of setting. Whisk the egg whites until stiff, then whisk in the remaining caster sugar. Fold lightly but thoroughly into the cheese mixture. Spoon the mixture into the prepared tin and shake the tin gently to level the surface. Chill for 3–4 hours or until the filling is set. Carefully release the sides of the tin from the cheesecake and lift the set cheesecake out on the tin base. Cover the top of the cheesecake with the whipped cream. Press the marshmallow halves gently into the cream. Melt the chocolate in a small heatproof bowl over a pan of hot water. Put into a piping bag fitted with a fine plain 'writing' nozzle. Using very gentle pressure, shake the piping bag carefully backwards and forwards across the top of the cheesecake to give a 'spider's web' of chocolate. Chill.

Serves 8

Meringue cheesecake; Marshmallow cheesecake; Toffee apple cheesecake

Toffee apple cheesecake

Metric	Imperial
50 g butter or margarine	2 oz butter or margarine
50 g caster sugar	2 oz caster sugar
100 g oatcake biscuits, finely crumbled	4 oz oatcake biscuits, finely crumbled

Filling:

Metric	Imperial
225 g full fat soft cheese	8 oz full fat soft cheese
2 eggs, separated	2 eggs, separated
100 g caster sugar	4 oz caster sugar
grated rind and juice of ½ lemon	grated rind and juice of ½ lemon
150 ml soured cream	¼ pint soured cream
300 ml apple purée	½ pint apple purée
pinch of mixed spice	pinch of mixed spice
20 g powdered gelatine	¾ oz powdered gelatine
8 × 15 ml spoons apple juice	8 tablespoons apple juice

Topping:

Metric	Imperial
75 g sugar	3 oz sugar
3 × 15 ml spoons water	3 tablespoons water
150 ml double or whipping cream, whipped	¼ pint double or whipping cream, whipped
1 dessert apple, cored and sliced	1 dessert apple, cored and sliced

Preparation time: 1 hour 20 minutes (plus chilling)

Melt the butter or margarine and sugar in a saucepan and stir in the oatcake biscuit crumbs. Press evenly over the bottom of a greased loose-bottomed 18–20 cm/7–8 inch round cake tin. Chill. Soften the cheese in a large mixing bowl. Beat in the egg yolks, 50 g/2 oz of the caster sugar, the lemon rind and juice, soured cream, apple purée and spice. Put the gelatine and apple juice into a small heatproof bowl over a saucepan of hot water and stir until the gelatine has dissolved. Beat the gelatine into the cheese mixture. Leave on one side until the mixture is on the point of setting. Whisk the egg whites until stiff, then whisk in the remaining caster sugar. Fold lightly but thoroughly into the cheese mixture. Spoon the mixture into the prepared tin and shake the tin gently to level the surface. Chill for 3–4 hours or until the filling is set. For the topping, put the sugar and water into a small saucepan and stir over a gentle heat until the sugar has dissolved. Bring to the boil and boil gently until the sugar and water turn to a thick golden syrup. Remove from the heat and allow to cool. Stir in the double cream and chill. Carefully release the sides of the tin from the cheesecake and lift the set cheesecake out on the tin base. Top with the toffee-flavoured cream and decorate with apple slices.

Serves 8

Primrose cheesecake

Preparation time: 1¼ hours (plus chilling)

Metric
50 g butter or margarine
50 g caster sugar
100 g chocolate-coated
  digestive biscuits, finely
  crushed

Imperial
2 oz butter or margarine
2 oz caster sugar
4 oz chocolate-coated
  digestive biscuits, finely
  crushed

Filling:
275 g full fat soft cheese
2 eggs, separated
2 egg yolks
100 g caster sugar
150 ml soured cream
few drops of yellow food
  colouring
15 g powdered gelatine
3 × 15 ml spoons water
2 × 15 ml spoons advocaat

Filling:
10 oz full fat soft cheese
2 eggs, separated
2 egg yolks
4 oz caster sugar
¼ pint soured cream
few drops of yellow food
  colouring
½ oz powdered gelatine
3 tablespoons water
2 tablespoons advocaat

Topping:
150 ml double or whipping
  cream, whipped
few drops of yellow food
  colouring (optional)
sugared jelly sweets
few split blanched almonds

Topping:
¼ pint double or whipping
  cream, whipped
few drops of yellow food
  colouring (optional)
sugared jelly sweets
few split blanched almonds

Melt the butter or margarine and sugar in a saucepan over a gentle heat and stir in the biscuit crumbs. Press evenly over the bottom of a greased loose-bottomed 18–20 cm/7–8 inch round cake tin. Chill.

Soften the cheese in a large mixing bowl. Beat in the 4 egg yolks, 50 g/2 oz of the caster sugar, the soured cream and a few drops of yellow food colouring. Put the gelatine and water into a small heatproof bowl over a saucepan of hot water and stir until the gelatine has dissolved. Beat the gelatine into the cheese mixture, together with the advocaat. Leave on one side until the mixture is on the point of setting.

Whisk the egg whites until stiff, then whisk in the remaining caster sugar. Fold lightly but thoroughly into the cheese mixture. Spoon the mixture into the prepared tin and shake the tin gently to level the surface. Chill for 3–4 hours or until the filling is set. Carefully release the sides of the tin from the cheesecake and lift the set cheesecake out on the tin base. Mix the whipped cream with sufficient yellow food colouring (if using) to give a deep 'daffodil' yellow. Swirl over the top of the cheesecake. Decorate with sugared jelly sweets and split blanched almonds.
Serves 8

Chocolate chip cheesecake; Iced melon cheesecake;
Primrose cheesecake

Iced melon cheesecake

Metric	Imperial
50 g butter or margarine	2 oz butter or margarine
50 g caster sugar	2 oz caster sugar
100 g gingernut biscuits, finely crushed	4 oz gingernut biscuits, finely crushed

Filling:

½ medium, ripe Charentais melon, peeled, seeded and cubed	½ medium, ripe Charentais melon, peeled, seeded and cubed
275 g full fat soft cheese	10 oz full fat soft cheese
2 eggs, separated	2 eggs, separated
100 g caster sugar	4 oz caster sugar
grated rind and juice of ½ lemon	grated rind and juice of ½ lemon
150 ml double or whipping cream	¼ pint double or whipping cream
20 g powdered gelatine	¾ oz powdered gelatine
5 × 15 ml spoons sweet white wine	5 tablespoons sweet white wine

Topping:

150 ml soured cream	¼ pint soured cream
yellow food colouring	yellow food colouring
small chocolate mint sticks	small chocolate mint sticks

Preparation time: 1 hour 25 minutes (plus chilling)

Melt the butter or margarine and sugar in a saucepan over a gentle heat and stir in the biscuit crumbs. Press evenly over the bottom of a greased loose-bottomed 18–20 cm/7–8 inch round cake tin. Chill while you make the filling.

Put the melon cubes into the blender goblet and blend to a smooth purée. Soften the cheese in a large mixing bowl. Beat in the egg yolks, 50 g/2 oz of the caster sugar, the lemon rind and juice, cream and the melon purée. Put the gelatine and wine into a small heatproof bowl over a saucepan of hot water and stir until the gelatine has dissolved. Beat the gelatine into the cheese mixture. Leave on one side until the mixture is on the point of setting.

Whisk the egg whites until stiff, then whisk in the remaining caster sugar. Fold lightly but thoroughly into the cheese mixture. Spoon the mixture into the prepared tin and shake the tin gently to level the surface. Chill for 1 hour.

For the topping, mix the soured cream with a few drops of yellow food colouring to tint it pale yellow. Spoon evenly over the top of the cheesecake. Put into the freezer and freeze for 1 hour. The cheesecake should still be slightly frozen when served, rather like a sorbet. Carefully release the sides of the tin from the cheesecake and lift the semi-frozen cheesecake out on the tin base. Top with the small chocolate mint sticks and serve immediately. The cheesecake will cut more easily if the knife is first dipped into hot water.

Serves 8

Chocolate chip cheesecake

Metric	Imperial
50 g butter or margarine	2 oz butter or margarine
50 g caster sugar	2 oz caster sugar
100 g chocolate-coated digestive biscuits, finely crushed	4 oz chocolate-coated digestive biscuits, finely crushed

Filling:

225 g full fat soft cheese	8 oz full fat soft cheese
2 eggs, separated	2 eggs, separated
50 g soft brown sugar	2 oz soft brown sugar
150 ml chocolate-flavoured yogurt	¼ pint chocolate-flavoured yogurt
15 g powdered gelatine	½ oz powdered gelatine
5 × 15 ml spoons water	5 tablespoons water
50 g caster sugar	2 oz caster sugar
100 g plain chocolate, cut into small pieces, or chocolate chips (see below)	4 oz plain chocolate, cut into small pieces, or chocolate chips (see below)

Topping:

150 ml double or whipping cream, whipped	¼ pint double or whipping cream, whipped
1 large chocolate flake bar	1 large chocolate flake bar

Preparation time: 1 hour 20 minutes (plus chilling)

Chocolate can be bought in 'chip' form – as small buttons, in shreds, etc., and any of these products are suitable for using in the cheesecake filling.

Melt the butter or margarine and sugar in a saucepan over a gentle heat and stir in the biscuit crumbs. Press evenly over the bottom of a greased loose-bottomed 18–20 cm/7–8 inch round cake tin. Chill while you make the filling.

Soften the cheese in a large mixing bowl. Beat in the egg yolks, soft brown sugar and yogurt. Put the gelatine and water into a small heatproof bowl over a saucepan of hot water and stir until the gelatine has dissolved. Beat the gelatine into the cheese mixture. Leave on one side until the mixture is on the point of setting.

Whisk the egg whites until stiff, then whisk in the caster sugar. Fold lightly but thoroughly into the cheese mixture, together with the pieces of chocolate. Spoon the mixture into the prepared tin and shake the tin gently to level the surface. Chill for 3–4 hours or until the filling is set.

Carefully release the sides of the tin from the cheesecake and lift the set cheesecake out on the tin base. Decorate the top of the cheesecake with piped whipped cream. Using a small sharp knife cut the flake bar into long thin shreds and sprinkle over the cheesecake.

Serves 8

Strawberry cheesecake

Metric	Imperial
2 thin sponge layers, 18–20 cm in diameter and 1 cm thick	2 thin sponge layers, 7–8 inches in diameter and ½ inch thick

Filling:

Metric	Imperial
8–10 large strawberries, hulled and halved	8–10 large strawberries, hulled and halved
225 g full fat soft cheese	8 oz full fat soft cheese
2 eggs, separated	2 eggs, separated
100 g caster sugar	4 oz caster sugar
few drops of vanilla essence	few drops of vanilla essence
150 ml double or whipping cream	¼ pint double or whipping cream
3 × 15 ml spoons strawberry jam	3 tablespoons strawberry jam
15 g powdered gelatine	½ oz powdered gelatine
4 × 15 ml spoons water	4 tablespoons water

Topping:

Metric	Imperial
225 g icing sugar	8 oz icing sugar
1 egg white	1 egg white
gravy browning	gravy browning

Preparation time: 1 hour 20 minutes (plus chilling)

Place one sponge layer in a greased loose-bottomed 18–20 cm/7–8 inch round cake tin.

To make the filling, arrange the strawberry halves upright on the sponge around the inside edge of the cake tin – the cut surfaces of the strawberries should be against the side of the tin. Soften the cheese in a large mixing bowl. Beat in the egg yolks, 50 g/2 oz of the caster sugar, the vanilla essence, cream and strawberry jam. Put the gelatine and water into a small heatproof bowl over a saucepan of hot water and stir until the gelatine has dissolved. Beat the gelatine into the cheese mixture. Leave on one side until the mixture is on the point of setting.

Whisk the egg whites until stiff, then whisk in the remaining caster sugar. Fold lightly but thoroughly into the cheese mixture. Spoon the mixture into the prepared tin, taking care not to disturb the strawberries. Shake the tin very gently to level the surface. Place the second sponge layer on top of the filling. Chill for 3–4 hours or until set.

Sift the icing sugar into a bowl. Whisk the egg white until fluffy and stir into the icing sugar. Add sufficient hot water to give a coating consistency, beating until smooth. Tint a small amount of the icing a chocolate colour with a few drops of gravy browning. Carefully release the sides of the tin from the cheesecake and lift the set cheesecake out on the tin base. Spread the white icing in a thin layer over the top of the cheesecake. Using a piping bag and a small 'writing' nozzle, pipe a design of chocolate-coloured icing on top of the white icing. Chill for a further 30 minutes.

Serves 8

Peach melba cheesecake

Metric	Imperial
1 thin sponge layer, 18–20 cm in diameter and 1 cm thick	1 thin sponge layer, 7–8 inches in diameter and ½ inch thick

Filling:

Metric	Imperial
1 × 425 g can peach slices, drained	1 × 15 oz can peach slices, drained
grated rind and juice of ½ orange	grated rind and juice of ½ orange
225 g full fat soft cheese	8 oz full fat soft cheese
2 eggs, separated	2 eggs, separated
100 g caster sugar	4 oz caster sugar
150 ml soured cream	¼ pint soured cream
20 g powdered gelatine	¾ oz powdered gelatine
6 × 15 ml spoons water	6 tablespoons water

Topping:

Metric	Imperial
150 ml double or whipping cream, whipped	¼ pint double or whipping cream, whipped
1 × 425 g can peach slices, drained	1 × 15 oz can peach slices, drained
3 × 15 ml spoons raspberry jam	3 tablespoons raspberry jam
1 × 15 ml spoon brandy	1 tablespoon brandy

Preparation time: 1½ hours (plus chilling)

Place the sponge layer in a greased loose-bottomed 18–20 cm/7–8 inch round cake tin, trimming the cake if necessary so that it fits in the bottom of the tin exactly.

To make the filling, put the peach slices into the blender goblet with the orange rind and juice and blend to a smooth purée. Soften the cheese in a large mixing bowl. Beat in the egg yolks, 50 g/2 oz of the caster sugar, the soured cream and the peach purée. Put the gelatine and water into a small heatproof bowl over a saucepan of hot water and stir until the gelatine has dissolved. Beat the gelatine into the cheese mixture. Leave on one side until the mixture is on the point of setting.

Whisk the egg whites until stiff, then whisk in the remaining caster sugar. Fold lightly but thoroughly into the cheese mixture. Spoon the mixture into the prepared tin and shake the tin gently to level the surface. Chill for 3–4 hours or until the filling is set. Carefully release the sides of the tin from the cheesecake and lift the set cheesecake out on the tin base. Spread or pipe the whipped cream on top of the cheesecake, and top with the peach slices. Put the raspberry jam and brandy into a small saucepan and heat gently until melted. Push through a sieve. Allow to cool, then spoon the melba sauce over the peaches and cream.

Serves 8

Strawberry cheesecake; Peach melba cheesecake

Pineapple rice cheesecake

Metric	Imperial
50 g butter or margarine	2 oz butter or margarine
50 g caster sugar	2 oz caster sugar
75 g digestive biscuits, finely crushed	3 oz digestive biscuits, finely crushed
25 g nuts, chopped	1 oz nuts, chopped
generous pinch of mixed spice	generous pinch of mixed spice

Filling:

Metric	Imperial
1 × 100 g packet pineapple jelly	1 × 4 oz packet pineapple jelly
150 ml boiling water	¼ pint boiling water
225 g full fat soft cheese	8 oz full fat soft cheese
2 eggs, separated	2 eggs, separated
100 g caster sugar	4 oz caster sugar
1 × 200 g can creamed rice pudding	1 × 7 oz can creamed rice pudding
50 g glacé pineapple, chopped (optional)	2 oz glacé pineapple, chopped (optional)

Topping:

Metric	Imperial
1 egg white, stiffly whisked	1 egg white, stiffly whisked
150 ml double or whipping cream, whipped	¼ pint double or whipping cream, whipped
50 g glacé pineapple, chopped	2 oz glacé pineapple, chopped
6 maraschino cherries, chopped	6 maraschino cherries, chopped

Preparation time: 1 hour 35 minutes (plus chilling)

Melt the butter or margarine and sugar in a saucepan over a gentle heat and stir in the biscuit crumbs, nuts and spice. Press evenly over the bottom of a greased loose-bottomed 18–20 cm/7–8 inch round cake tin. Chill while you make the filling.

Cut the jelly tablet into small pieces with kitchen scissors. Put the jelly into a bowl and add the boiling water. Stir until completely melted, then allow to cool. Soften the cheese in a large mixing bowl. Beat in the egg yolks, 50 g/2 oz of the caster sugar, the canned rice pudding and the melted jelly. Leave on one side until the mixture is on the point of setting.

Whisk the egg whites until stiff, then whisk in the remaining caster sugar. Fold lightly but thoroughly into the cheese mixture, together with the chopped glacé pineapple, if used. Spoon the mixture into the prepared tin and shake the tin gently to level the surface. Chill for 3–4 hours or until the filling is set. Carefully release the sides of the tin from the cheesecake and lift the set cheesecake out on the tin base. Fold the whisked egg white into the whipped cream, with the chopped pineapple and maraschino cherries. Spread over the top of the cheesecake.
Serves 8

Mandarin cheesecake

Metric	Imperial
24 sponge fingers	24 sponge fingers

Filling:

Metric	Imperial
1 × 300 g can mandarin oranges	1 × 11 oz can mandarin oranges
225 g full fat soft cheese	8 oz full fat soft cheese
2 eggs, separated	2 eggs, separated
100 g caster sugar	4 oz caster sugar
150 ml soured cream	¼ pint soured cream
15 g powdered gelatine	½ oz powdered gelatine

Topping:

Metric	Imperial
150 ml double or whipping cream, whipped	¼ pint double or whipping cream, whipped
1 × 300 g can mandarin oranges, drained	1 × 11 oz can mandarin oranges, drained

Preparation time: 1 hour 20 minutes (plus chilling)

Trim one end from each sponge finger so that the fingers are 7.5 cm/3 inches long. Completely line the sides of a generously greased loose-bottomed 18–20 cm/7–8 inch round cake tin with sponge fingers standing upright. Use the remaining fingers and some of the trimmings to line the bottom of the tin.

To make the filling, drain the mandarin oranges, reserving the juice. Arrange the mandarin oranges on top of the sponge fingers in the bottom of the tin. Soften the cheese in a large mixing bowl. Beat in the egg yolks, 50 g/2 oz of the caster sugar and the soured cream. Put the gelatine and 5 × 15 ml spoons/5 tablespoons of the reserved mandarin juice in a heatproof bowl over a saucepan of hot water and stir until the gelatine has dissolved. Beat the gelatine into the cheese mixture. Leave on one side until the mixture is on the point of setting.

Whisk the egg whites until stiff, then whisk in the remaining caster sugar. Fold lightly but thoroughly into the cheese mixture. Spoon the mixture into the prepared tin and shake the tin gently to level the surface. Chill for 3–4 hours or until the filling is set. For the topping, combine the whipped cream with the mandarin oranges. Spoon on top of the cheesecake and chill for a further 30 minutes.

Carefully release the sides of the tin from the cheesecake and lift the set cheesecake out on the tin base.
Serves 8

Neapolitan layered cheesecake

Metric
50 g butter or margarine
50 g caster sugar
100 g chocolate-covered
  digestive biscuits, finely
  crushed

Filling:
350 g full fat soft cheese
3 eggs, separated
175 g caster sugar
200 ml double or whipping
  cream
20 g powdered gelatine
8 × 15 ml spoons water
vanilla essence
green food colouring
peppermint essence
cochineal
raspberry essence

Topping:
150 ml double or whipping
  cream, whipped
hundreds and thousands or
  small jelly sweets

Imperial
2 oz butter or margarine
2 oz caster sugar
4 oz chocolate-covered
  digestive biscuits, finely
  crushed

Filling:
12 oz full fat soft cheese
3 eggs, separated
6 oz caster sugar
⅓ pint double or whipping
  cream
¾ oz powdered gelatine
8 tablespoons water
vanilla essence
green food colouring
peppermint essence
cochineal
raspberry essence

Topping:
¼ pint double or whipping
  cream, whipped
hundreds and thousands or
  small jelly sweets

Preparation time: 1 hour 35 minutes (plus chilling)

This would make an ideal cake to serve for a children's birthday party.

Melt the butter or margarine and sugar in a saucepan over a gentle heat and stir in the biscuit crumbs. Press evenly over the bottom of a greased loose-bottomed 18–20 cm/7–8 inch round cake tin. Chill.
Soften the cheese in a large mixing bowl. Beat in the egg yolks, 50 g/2 oz of the caster sugar and the cream. Put the gelatine and water into a small heatproof bowl over a saucepan of hot water and stir until the gelatine has dissolved. Beat the gelatine into the cheese mixture.
Divide the cheese mixture into three equal portions, putting each one into a separate bowl. Add a few drops of vanilla essence to one portion; add a few drops of green food colouring and peppermint essence to the second portion; and add a few drops of cochineal and raspberry essence to the third portion. Leave on one side until the mixtures are on the point of setting.
Whisk the egg whites until stiff, then whisk in the remaining caster sugar. Fold one-third of the egg whites into each portion of the cheese mixture. Spoon the pink mixture into the prepared tin and shake the tin to level the surface. Spoon the vanilla mixture carefully over the top and level it with the back of the spoon. Finally spoon the green mixture over the vanilla one and level it with the back of the spoon. Chill for 3–4 hours or until the filling is set.
Carefully release the sides of the tin from the cheese-cake and lift the cheesecake out on the tin base. Decorate with the cream, piped on top, and hundreds and thousands or jelly sweets.
Serves 8–10

Pineapple rice cheesecake; Neapolitan layered cheesecake;
Mandarin cheesecake

Banana cheesecake

Preparation time: 1 hour 25 minutes (plus chilling)

Metric
50 g butter or margarine
50 g caster sugar
100 g chocolate-coated
  digestive biscuits, finely
  crushed

Imperial
2 oz butter or margarine
2 oz caster sugar
4 oz chocolate-coated
  digestive biscuits, finely
  crushed

Filling:
2 ripe bananas, peeled
grated rind and juice of ½
  lemon
100 g caster sugar
225 g full fat soft cheese
2 eggs, separated
150 ml soured cream
15 g powdered gelatine
5 × 15 ml spoons water

Filling:
2 ripe bananas, peeled
grated rind and juice of ½
  lemon
4 oz caster sugar
8 oz full fat soft cheese
2 eggs, separated
¼ pint soured cream
½ oz powdered gelatine
5 tablespoons water

Topping:
150 ml double or whipping
  cream, whipped
2 bananas, peeled and
  thinly sliced
juice of 1 lemon

Topping:
¼ pint double or whipping
  cream, whipped
2 bananas, peeled and
  thinly sliced
juice of 1 lemon

Melt the butter or margarine and sugar in a saucepan over a gentle heat and stir in the biscuit crumbs. Press evenly over the bottom of a greased loose-bottomed 18–20 cm/7–8 inch round cake tin. Chill while you make the filling.

Put the bananas into a large mixing bowl with the lemon rind and juice and 50 g/2 oz of the caster sugar. Mash until smooth. Beat in the cheese, egg yolks and soured cream. Put the gelatine and water into a small heatproof bowl over a saucepan of hot water and stir until the gelatine has dissolved. Beat the gelatine into the cheese mixture. Leave on one side until the mixture is on the point of setting.

Whisk the egg whites until stiff, then whisk in the remaining caster sugar. Fold lightly but thoroughly into the cheese mixture.

Spoon the mixture into the prepared tin and shake the tin gently to level the surface. Chill for 3–4 hours or until the filling is set.

Carefully release the sides of the tin from the cheesecake and lift the set cheesecake out on the tin base. Pipe the cream on top of the cheesecake. Dip the banana slices into lemon juice to prevent them discolouring and arrange on the cream.
Serves 8

Jellied raspberry cheesecake

Metric
1 large or 2 small jam-filled
  Swiss rolls, thinly sliced

Filling:
1 packet raspberry jelly
225 g full fat soft cheese
2 eggs, separated
100 g caster sugar
150 ml double or whipping
  cream

Imperial
1 large or 2 small jam-filled
  Swiss rolls, thinly sliced

Filling:
1 packet raspberry jelly
8 oz full fat soft cheese
2 eggs, separated
4 oz caster sugar
$\frac{1}{4}$ pint double or whipping
  cream

Preparation time: 1½ hours (plus chilling)

This cheesecake looks very attractive just with its simple jelly topping. However, it can also be decorated with whipped cream and fresh or frozen raspberries.

Line the bottom and sides of a greased loose-bottomed 18–20 cm/7–8 inch round cake tin with the Swiss roll slices. If the tin has been greased well the Swiss roll slices should stand quite easily around the sides.
To make the filling, cut the jelly tablet into small pieces with kitchen scissors. Put the jelly into a bowl and add 150 ml/¼ pint boiling water. Stir until completely melted, then allow to cool. Soften the cheese in a large mixing bowl. Beat in the egg yolks, 50 g/2 oz of the caster sugar, the cream and all but 3 × 15 ml spoons/3 tablespoons of the melted jelly. Leave on one side until the mixture is on the point of setting.
Whisk the egg whites until stiff, then whisk in the remaining caster sugar. Fold lightly but thoroughly into the cheese mixture. Spoon the mixture into the prepared tin and shake the tin gently to level the surface. Chill for 1 hour or until the filling is set.
Mix the reserved, now set jelly with 3 × 15 ml spoons/3 tablespoons boiling water and stir until liquid. Allow to cool, then spoon evenly over the top of the set cheesecake. Chill for a further 2–3 hours.
Carefully release the sides of the tin from the cheesecake and lift the set cheesecake out on the tin base.
Serves 8

Banana cheesecake; Jellied raspberry cheesecake; Green goddess cheesecake

Green goddess cheesecake

Metric
1 thin sponge layer, 18–
  20 cm in diameter and
  1 cm thick

Filling:
225 g full fat soft cheese
2 eggs, separated
100 g caster sugar
150 ml double or whipping
  cream
2 × 15 ml spoons crème de
  menthe
15 g powdered gelatine
5 × 15 ml spoons water
50 g pistachios, chopped

Topping:
150 ml double or whipping
  cream
green food colouring
thin matchstick strips of
  angelica
few halved pistachio nuts

Imperial
1 thin sponge layer, 7–8
  inches in diameter and ½
  inch thick

Filling:
8 oz full fat soft cheese
2 eggs, separated
4 oz caster sugar
¼ pint double or whipping
  cream
2 tablespoons crème de
  menthe
½ oz powdered gelatine
5 tablespoons water
2 oz pistachios, chopped

Topping:
¼ pint double or whipping
  cream
green food colouring
thin matchstick strips of
  angelica
few halved pistachio nuts

Preparation time: 1 hour 10 minutes (plus chilling)

Place the sponge layer in a greased loose-bottomed 18–20 cm/7–8 inch round cake tin, trimming the cake if necessary so that it fits in the bottom of the tin exactly.
To make the filling, soften the cheese in a large mixing bowl. Beat in the egg yolks, 50 g/2 oz of the caster sugar, the cream and crème de menthe. Put the gelatine and water into a small heatproof bowl over a saucepan of hot water and stir until the gelatine has dissolved. Beat the gelatine into the cheese mixture. Leave on one side until the mixture is on the point of setting.
Whisk the egg whites until stiff, then whisk in the remaining caster sugar. Fold lightly but thoroughly into the cheese mixture, together with the chopped pistachios. Spoon the mixture into the prepared tin and shake the tin gently to level the surface. Chill for 3–4 hours or until the filling is set.
Carefully release the sides of the tin from the cheesecake and lift the set cheesecake out on the tin base. Whip the cream until thick with a little green food colouring to tint it pale green. Pipe or swirl the cream on top of the cheesecake. Decorate with strips of angelica and pistachios.
Serves 8

Pumpkin cheesecake

Metric
50 g butter or margarine
50 g demerara sugar
100 g oatcake biscuits,
  finely crumbled

Filling:
225 g full fat soft cheese
2 eggs, separated
100 g dark soft brown sugar
grated rind of $\frac{1}{2}$ lemon
1 × 2.5 ml spoon ground
  ginger
generous pinch of ground
  cinnamon
150 ml soured cream
225 g canned puréed
  pumpkin
20 g powdered gelatine
8 × 15 ml spoons water
50 g caster sugar

Topping:
3 × 15 ml spoons clear
  honey
75 g walnuts, chopped

Imperial
2 oz butter or margarine
2 oz demerara sugar
4 oz oatcake biscuits, finely
  crumbled

Filling:
8 oz full fat soft cheese
2 eggs, separated
4 oz dark soft brown sugar
grated rind of $\frac{1}{2}$ lemon
$\frac{1}{2}$ teaspoon ground
  ginger
generous pinch of ground
  cinnamon
$\frac{1}{4}$ pint soured cream
8 oz canned puréed
  pumpkin
$\frac{3}{4}$ oz powdered gelatine
8 tablespoons water
2 oz caster sugar

Topping:
3 tablespoons clear
  honey
3 oz walnuts, chopped

Preparation time: $1\frac{1}{4}$ hours (plus chilling)

Melt the butter or margarine in a saucepan. Stir in the demerara sugar and oatcake biscuit crumbs. Press evenly over the bottom of a greased loose-bottomed 18–20 cm/7–8 inch round cake tin. Chill while you make the filling.

Soften the cheese in a large mixing bowl. Beat in the egg yolks, brown sugar, lemon rind, spices, soured cream and pumpkin purée. Put the gelatine and water into a small heatproof bowl over a saucepan of hot water and stir until the gelatine has dissolved. Beat the gelatine into the cheese mixture. Leave on one side until the mixture is on the point of setting.

Whisk the egg whites until stiff, then whisk in the caster sugar. Fold lightly but thoroughly into the cheese mixture. Spoon the mixture into the prepared tin and shake the tin gently to level the surface. Chill for 3–4 hours or until the filling is set.

Carefully release the sides of the tin from the cheesecake and lift the set cheesecake out on the tin base. Mix the honey and nuts together and spoon over the cheesecake.

Serves 8

Pumpkin cheesecake; Crab apple jelly cheesecake; Apricot cheesecake

Crab apple jelly cheesecake

Metric
50 g butter or margarine
50 g caster sugar
100 g digestive biscuits, finely crushed
generous pinch of mixed spice
generous pinch of grated nutmeg

Filling:
225 g full fat soft cheese
2 eggs, separated
100 g caster sugar
grated rind and juice of ½ lemon
150 ml double or whipping cream
4 × 15 ml spoons crab apple jelly (or other fruit jelly)
15 g powdered gelatine
5 × 15 ml spoons apple juice

Topping:
3 × 15 ml spoons crab apple jelly
150 ml double or whipping cream, whipped

Imperial
2 oz butter or margarine
2 oz caster sugar
4 oz digestive biscuits, finely crushed
generous pinch of mixed spice
generous pinch of grated nutmeg

Filling:
8 oz full fat soft cheese
2 eggs, separated
4 oz caster sugar
grated rind and juice of ½ lemon
¼ pint double or whipping cream
4 tablespoons crab apple jelly (or other fruit jelly)
½ oz powdered gelatine
5 tablespoons apple juice

Topping:
3 tablespoons crab apple jelly
¼ pint double or whipping cream, whipped

Preparation time: 1½ hours (plus chilling)

Melt the butter or margarine and sugar in a saucepan over a gentle heat and stir in the biscuit crumbs together with the spices. Press evenly over the bottom of a greased loose-bottomed 18–20 cm/7–8 inch round cake tin. Chill while you make the filling.
Soften the cheese in a large mixing bowl. Beat in the egg yolks, 50 g/2 oz of the caster sugar, the lemon rind and juice, cream and crab apple jelly. Put the gelatine and apple juice into a small heatproof bowl over a saucepan of hot water and stir until the gelatine has dissolved. Beat the gelatine into the cheese mixture. Leave on one side until the mixture is on the point of setting.
Whisk the egg whites until stiff, then whisk in the remaining caster sugar. Fold lightly but thoroughly into the cheese mixture. Spoon the mixture into the prepared tin and shake the tin gently to level the surface. Chill for 3–4 hours or until the filling is set.
Carefully release the sides of the tin from the cheesecake and lift the set cheesecake out on the tin base. Melt the crab apple jelly in a saucepan over a gentle heat. Allow to cool, then spread evenly over the top of the cheesecake and decorate with the cream.
Serves 8

Apricot cheesecake

Metric
50 g butter or margarine
50 g demerara sugar
100 g oatcake biscuits, finely crumbled

Filling:
175 g dried apricots, soaked overnight and drained
juice of 2 oranges
3 × 15 ml spoons honey
225 g full fat soft cheese
2 eggs, separated
100 g caster sugar
4 × 15 ml spoons soured cream
15 g powdered gelatine
5 × 15 ml spoons water
50 g ratafias, coarsely crumbled

Topping:
3 × 15 ml spoons apricot jam, melted
150 ml double or whipping cream, whipped
50 g ratafias

Imperial
2 oz butter or margarine
2 oz demerara sugar
4 oz oatcake biscuits, finely crumbled

Filling:
6 oz dried apricots, soaked overnight and drained
juice of 2 oranges
3 tablespoons honey
8 oz full fat soft cheese
2 eggs, separated
4 oz caster sugar
4 tablespoons soured cream
½ oz powdered gelatine
5 tablespoons water
2 oz ratafias, coarsely crumbled

Topping:
3 tablespoons apricot jam, melted
¼ pint double or whipping cream, whipped
2 oz ratafias

Preparation time: 1 hour 40 minutes (plus chilling)

Melt the butter or margarine in a saucepan. Stir in the demerara sugar and biscuit crumbs. Press evenly over the bottom of a greased loose-bottomed 18–20 cm/7–8 inch round cake tin. Chill while you make the filling. Put the apricots into a saucepan with the orange juice and honey. Cover and simmer gently until the apricots are just tender. Put the apricots and their juice into the blender goblet and blend until smooth. Allow to cool. Soften the cheese in a large mixing bowl. Beat in the egg yolks, 50 g/2 oz of the caster sugar, the soured cream and apricot purée. Put the gelatine and water into a small heatproof bowl over a saucepan of hot water and stir until the gelatine has dissolved. Beat the gelatine into the cheese mixture. Leave on one side until the mixture is on the point of setting.
Whisk the egg whites until stiff, then whisk in the remaining caster sugar. Fold lightly but thoroughly into the cheese mixture, together with the crumbled ratafias. Spoon the mixture into the prepared tin and shake the tin gently to level the surface. Chill for 3–4 hours or until the filling is set.
Carefully release the sides of the tin from the cheesecake and lift the set cheesecake out on the tin base. Spread the top of the cheesecake with a thin layer of melted apricot jam. Decorate with the whipped cream and ratafias.
Serves 8

Peanut and raisin cheesecake

Metric
50 g butter or margarine
25 g caster sugar
3 × 15 ml spoons golden
  syrup
75 g corn flakes
25 g unsalted peanuts,
  chopped

Filling:
225 g full fat soft cheese
4 × 15 ml spoons peanut
  butter
2 eggs, separated
100 g caster sugar
few drops of vanilla essence
150 ml plain unsweetened
  yogurt
15 g powdered gelatine
5 × 15 ml spoons water
50 g unsalted peanuts,
  chopped
50 g seedless raisins

Topping:
150 ml double cream,
  whipped
75 g chocolate-coated
  peanuts

Imperial
2 oz butter or margarine
1 oz caster sugar
3 tablespoons golden
  syrup
3 oz corn flakes
1 oz unsalted peanuts,
  chopped

Filling:
8 oz full fat soft cheese
4 tablespoons peanut
  butter
2 eggs, separated
4 oz caster sugar
few drops of vanilla essence
1/4 pint plain unsweetened
  yogurt
1/2 oz powdered gelatine
5 tablespoons water
2 oz unsalted peanuts,
  chopped
2 oz seedless raisins

Topping:
1/4 pint double cream,
  whipped
3 oz chocolate-coated
  peanuts

Preparation time: 1 hour 20 minutes (plus chilling)

Melt the butter or margarine, sugar and golden syrup in a saucepan over a gentle heat. Stir in the corn flakes and peanuts. Press evenly over the bottom of a greased loose-bottomed 18–20 cm/7–8 inch round cake tin. Chill while you make the filling.

Soften the cheese in a large mixing bowl. Beat in the peanut butter, egg yolks, 50 g/2 oz of the caster sugar, the vanilla essence and yogurt. Put the gelatine and water into a small heatproof bowl over a saucepan of hot water and stir until the gelatine has dissolved. Beat the gelatine into the cheese mixture. Put aside until the mixture is on the point of setting.

Whisk the egg whites until stiff, then whisk in the remaining caster sugar. Fold lightly but thoroughly into the cheese mixture, together with the chopped peanuts and raisins. Spoon the mixture into the prepared tin and shake the tin gently to level the surface. Chill for 3–4 hours or until the filling is set. Carefully release the sides of the tin from the cheesecake and lift the set cheesecake out on the tin base. Top the cheesecake with a cloud of whipped cream and sprinkle with the chocolate-coated peanuts.
Serves 8

Peanut and raisin cheesecake; Butterscotch Brazil cheesecake;
Maple peach cheesecake

Maple peach cheesecake

Metric
50 g butter or margarine
25 g caster sugar
3 × 15 ml spoons golden
  syrup
75 g puffed rice cereal

Filling:
1 × 425 g can peach slices,
  drained
3 × 15 ml spoons maple
  syrup
225 g full fat soft cheese
2 eggs, separated
100 g caster sugar
grated rind of ½ lemon
150 ml soured cream
20 g powdered gelatine
5 × 15 ml spoons water

Topping:
1 × 425 g can peach slices,
  drained
3 × 15 ml spoons maple
  syrup
50 g pecan or walnut halves

Imperial
2 oz butter or margarine
1 oz caster sugar
3 tablespoons golden
  syrup
3 oz puffed rice cereal

Filling:
1 × 15 oz can peach slices,
  drained
3 tablespoons maple
  syrup
8 oz full fat soft cheese
2 eggs, separated
4 oz caster sugar
grated rind of ½ lemon
¼ pint soured cream
¾ oz powdered gelatine
5 tablespoons water

Topping:
1 × 15 oz can peach slices,
  drained
3 tablespoons maple
  syrup
2 oz pecan or walnut halves

Preparation time: 1½ hours (plus chilling)

Melt the butter or margarine, sugar and golden syrup in a saucepan over a gentle heat. Stir in the puffed rice cereal. Press evenly over the bottom of a greased loose-bottomed 18–20 cm/7–8 inch round cake tin. Chill while you make the filling.
Put the peach slices into the blender goblet with the maple syrup and blend to a smooth purée. Soften the cheese in a large mixing bowl. Beat in the egg yolks, 50 g/2 oz of the caster sugar, the lemon rind, soured cream and peach purée. Put the gelatine and water into a small heatproof bowl over a saucepan of hot water and stir until the gelatine has dissolved. Beat the gelatine into the cheese mixture. Leave on one side until the mixture is on the point of setting.
Whisk the egg whites until stiff, then whisk in the remaining caster sugar. Fold lightly but thoroughly into the cheese mixture. Spoon the mixture into the prepared tin and shake the tin gently to level the surface. Chill for 3–4 hours or until the filling is set.
Carefully release the sides of the tin from the cheesecake and lift the set cheesecake out on the tin base. For the topping, cut the canned peach slices in two lengthways unless they are already very thin. Arrange overlapping slices of peach on top of the cheesecake. Spoon or brush the maple syrup over the peaches and decorate with the nuts.
Serves 8

Butterscotch Brazil cheesecake

Metric
50 g butter or margarine
50 g soft brown sugar
100 g digestive biscuits,
  finely crushed

Filling:
75 g buttered Brazil nuts
225 g full fat soft cheese
50 g soft brown sugar
2 eggs, separated
few drops of vanilla essence
150 ml double or whipping
  cream
15 g powdered gelatine
5 × 15 ml spoons water
50 g caster sugar

Topping:
150 ml soured cream
few drops of gravy
  browning
50 g buttered Brazil nuts

Imperial
2 oz butter or margarine
2 oz soft brown sugar
4 oz digestive biscuits,
  finely crushed

Filling:
3 oz buttered Brazil nuts
8 oz full fat soft cheese
2 oz soft brown sugar
2 eggs, separated
few drops of vanilla essence
¼ pint double or whipping
  cream
½ oz powdered gelatine
5 tablespoons water
2 oz caster sugar

Topping:
¼ pint soured cream
few drops of gravy
  browning
2 oz buttered Brazil nuts

Preparation time: 1 hour 20 minutes (plus chilling)

Melt the butter or margarine and brown sugar in a saucepan over a gentle heat and stir in the biscuit crumbs. Press evenly over the bottom of a greased loose-bottomed 18–20 cm/7–8 inch round cake tin. Chill while you make the filling.
Crush the buttered Brazil nuts coarsely with a rolling pin. Soften the cheese in a large mixing bowl. Beat in the brown sugar, egg yolks, vanilla essence and cream. Put the gelatine and water into a small heatproof bowl over a saucepan of hot water and stir until the gelatine has dissolved. Beat the gelatine into the cheese mixture. Leave on one side until the mixture is on the point of setting.
Whisk the egg whites until stiff, then whisk in the caster sugar. Fold lightly but thoroughly into the cheese mixture, together with the crushed Brazils. Spoon the mixture into the prepared tin and shake the tin gently to level the surface. Chill for 3–4 hours or until the filling is set.
Carefully release the sides of the tin from the cheesecake and lift the set cheesecake out on the tin base. Mix the soured cream with sufficient gravy browning to tint it a pale coffee colour. Spoon evenly over the top of the cheesecake and decorate with the buttered Brazils, either whole or crushed. The nuts may also be dipped in melted chocolate and then cocoa.
Serves 8

Seville cheesecake

Metric	Imperial
25 g butter or margarine	1 oz butter or margarine
50 g caster sugar	2 oz caster sugar
3 × 15 ml spoons jelly marmalade	3 tablespoons jelly marmalade
100 g digestive biscuits, finely crushed	4 oz digestive biscuits, finely crushed

Filling:

225 g full fat soft cheese	8 oz full fat soft cheese
2 eggs, separated	2 eggs, separated
grated rind of 2 oranges	grated rind of 2 oranges
100 g caster sugar	4 oz caster sugar
3 × 15 ml spoons coarse-cut marmalade, preferably Seville orange	3 tablespoons coarse-cut marmalade, preferably Seville orange
150 ml soured cream	¼ pint soured cream
15 g powdered gelatine	½ oz powdered gelatine
5 × 15 ml spoons water	5 tablespoons water

Topping:

2 oranges (use those left from the filling)	2 oranges (use those left from the filling)
3 × 15 ml spoons jelly marmalade	3 tablespoons jelly marmalade

Preparation time: 1 hour 35 minutes (plus chilling)

Melt the butter or margarine, sugar and marmalade in a saucepan over a gentle heat and stir in the biscuit crumbs. Press evenly over the bottom of a greased loose-bottomed 18–20 cm/7–8 inch round cake tin. Chill while you make the filling.
Soften the cheese in a large mixing bowl. Beat in the egg yolks, grated orange rind, 50 g/2 oz of the caster sugar, the marmalade and soured cream. Put the gelatine and water into a small heatproof bowl over a saucepan of hot water and stir until the gelatine has dissolved. Beat the gelatine into the cheese mixture. Leave on one side until the mixture is on the point of setting.
Whisk the egg whites until stiff, then whisk in the remaining caster sugar. Fold lightly but thoroughly into the cheese mixture. Spoon the mixture into the prepared tin and shake the tin gently to level the surface. Chill for 3–4 hours or until the filling is set. Carefully release the sides of the tin from the cheesecake and lift the set cheesecake out on the tin base. Remove all the pith from the 'grated' oranges and cut the oranges into thin slices, removing any loose pips. Arrange the orange slices decoratively on top of the cheesecake. Heat the jelly marmalade in a small saucepan until it is smooth and of a coating consistency. Cool slightly, then spoon over the orange slices to give a thin glaze. Chill to set the glaze before serving.
Serves 8

Cranberry and orange cheesecake

Metric	Imperial
50 g butter or margarine	2 oz butter or margarine
50 g caster sugar	2 oz caster sugar
100 g chocolate-coated digestive biscuits, finely crushed	4 oz chocolate-coated digestive biscuits, finely crushed
grated rind of 1 orange	grated rind 1 orange

Filling:

225 g full fat soft cheese	8 oz full fat soft cheese
2 eggs, separated	2 eggs, separated
175 g caster sugar	6 oz caster sugar
grated rind of 1–2 oranges	grated rind of 1–2 oranges
1 × 175 g jar cranberry sauce	1 × 6 oz jar cranberry sauce
150 ml soured cream	¼ pint soured cream
20 g powdered gelatine	¾ oz powdered gelatine
5 × 15 ml spoons water	5 tablespoons water

Topping:

150 ml double or whipping cream, whipped	¼ pint double or whipping cream, whipped
1 × 175 g jar cranberry sauce	1 × 6 oz jar cranberry sauce
1 × 300 g can mandarin oranges, drained	1 × 11 oz can mandarin oranges, drained

Preparation time: 1 hour 25 minutes (plus chilling)

Melt the butter or margarine and sugar in a saucepan over a gentle heat and stir in the biscuit crumbs and orange rind. Press evenly over the bottom of a greased loose-bottomed 18–20 cm/7–8 inch round cake tin. Chill while you make the filling.
Soften the cheese in a large mixing bowl. Beat in the egg yolks, 75 g/3 oz of the caster sugar, the orange rind, cranberry sauce and soured cream. Put the gelatine and water into a small heatproof bowl over a saucepan of hot water and stir until the gelatine has dissolved. Beat the gelatine into the cheese mixture. Leave on one side until the mixture is on the point of setting.
Whisk the egg whites until stiff, then whisk in the remaining caster sugar. Fold lightly but thoroughly into the cheese mixture. Spoon the mixture into the prepared tin and shake the tin gently to level the surface. Chill for 3–4 hours or until the filling is set. Carefully release the sides of the tin from the cheesecake and lift the set cheesecake out on the tin base. Pipe the whipped cream on top of the cheesecake, dividing it into 6 or 8 equal sections. Fill alternate sections with cranberry sauce and mandarin oranges.
Serves 8

Cranberry and orange cheesecake; Seville cheesecake; Lime marmalade cheesecake

Lime marmalade cheesecake

Preparation time: 1 hour 35 minutes (plus chilling)

Metric	**Imperial**
50 g butter or margarine	2 oz butter or margarine
50 g caster sugar	2 oz caster sugar
100 g gingernut biscuits, finely crushed	4 oz gingernut biscuits, finely crushed

Filling:

Metric	**Imperial**
225 g full fat soft cheese	8 oz full fat soft cheese
2 eggs, separated	2 eggs, separated
100 g caster sugar	4 oz caster sugar
grated rind and juice of 1 lemon	grated rind and juice of 1 lemon
150 ml double or whipping cream	¼ pint double or whipping cream
4 × 15 ml spoons lime marmalade	4 tablespoons lime marmalade
15 g powdered gelatine	½ oz powdered gelatine
4 × 15 ml spoons water	4 tablespoons water

Topping:

Metric	**Imperial**
4 × 15 ml spoons lime marmalade	4 tablespoons lime marmalade
50 g toasted nuts, chopped	2 oz toasted nuts, chopped
whipped cream (optional)	whipped cream (optional)

Melt the butter or margarine and sugar in a saucepan over a gentle heat and stir in the biscuit crumbs. Press evenly over the bottom of a greased loose-bottomed 18–20 cm/7–8 inch round cake tin. Chill while you make the filling.

Soften the cheese in a large mixing bowl. Beat in the egg yolks, 50 g/2 oz of the caster sugar, the lemon rind and juice, cream and lime marmalade. Put the gelatine and water into a small heatproof bowl over a saucepan of hot water and stir until the gelatine has dissolved. Beat the gelatine into the cheese mixture. Leave on one side until the mixture is on the point of setting. Whisk the egg whites until stiff, then whisk in the remaining caster sugar. Fold lightly but thoroughly into the cheese mixture. Spoon the mixture into the prepared tin and shake the tin gently to level the surface. Chill for 3–4 hours or until the filling is set. Carefully release the sides of the tin from the cheese-cake and lift the set cheesecake out on the tin base. Warm the lime marmalade gently until it is of a soft spreading consistency. Cool slightly, then spread over the top and sides of the cheesecake. Coat the sides of the cheesecake evenly with the chopped toasted nuts. For additional decoration, pipe with a little whipped cream.

Serves 8

SAVOURY CHEESECAKES

Surprisingly, a cheesecake need not necessarily be sweet, and, as this section illustrates, some of the best cheesecakes are savoury! All the cheeses that are used in cheesecakes are relatively bland, and it is very easy to switch the basic flavour one way or the other.

A savoury cheesecake makes a pleasant alternative to a cheese flan, and is just as convenient to serve, cut in wedges, with salad.

Spinach cheesecake

Metric	Imperial
75 g butter or margarine	3 oz butter or margarine
175 g water biscuits, finely crushed	6 oz water biscuits, finely crushed
salt	salt
freshly ground black pepper	freshly ground black pepper

Filling:

Metric	Imperial
1 × 225 g packet frozen chopped spinach, thawed	1 × 8 oz packet frozen chopped spinach, thawed
275 g full fat soft cheese	10 oz full fat soft cheese
3 eggs, separated	3 eggs, separated
grated rind of 1 lemon	grated rind of 1 lemon
30 g plain flour	1 oz plain flour
pinch of grated nutmeg	pinch of grated nutmeg
150 ml soured cream	¼ pint soured cream
salt	salt
freshly ground black pepper	freshly ground black pepper

Topping:

Metric	Imperial
150 ml soured cream	¼ pint soured cream
2 hard-boiled eggs, sliced	2 hard-boiled eggs, sliced
chopped fresh parsley	chopped fresh parsley

Preparation time: 45 minutes
Cooking time: 1½–1¾ hours
Oven: 160°C, 325°F, Gas Mark 3

Fresh spinach may be used for the filling when available; you will need about 450 g/1 lb.

Melt the butter or margarine in a saucepan over a gentle heat and stir in the biscuit crumbs with salt and pepper to taste. Press evenly over the bottom of a greased loose-bottomed 18–20 cm/7–8 inch round cake tin. Chill while you make the filling.
Press the thawed spinach firmly in a sieve to extract as much moisture as possible; this is very important as excess liquid will upset the balance of the recipe. Soften the cheese in a large mixing bowl. Beat in the egg yolks, lemon rind, flour, nutmeg, soured cream and salt and pepper to taste. Stir in the squeezed out spinach. Whisk the egg whites until stiff and fold lightly but thoroughly into the cheese mixture. Spoon the mixture into the prepared tin and smooth the surface level. Bake in a preheated oven for 1½–1¾ hours or until firm but still spongy to the touch.
To serve the cheesecake hot, heat the soured cream through gently. Ease the sides of the tin carefully away from the cheesecake and lift the hot cooked cheesecake out on the tin base. Top with the egg slices, spoon over the warm soured cream and sprinkle with parsley.
If you are going to serve the cheesecake cold, leave it to cool in the turned-off oven for 1 hour. Top with the soured cream, hard-boiled eggs and parsley, and chill.
Serves 6–8

Spinach cheesecake; Ham cheesecake

Ham cheesecake

Metric	Imperial
75 g butter or margarine	3 oz butter or margarine
175 g digestive biscuits, finely crushed	6 oz digestive biscuits, finely crushed
25 g Parmesan cheese, grated	1 oz Parmesan cheese, grated
salt	salt
freshly ground black pepper	freshly ground black pepper

Filling:

Metric	Imperial
225 g full fat soft cheese	8 oz full fat soft cheese
2 eggs, separated	2 eggs, separated
100 g cooked ham, minced or finely chopped	4 oz cooked ham, minced or finely chopped
1 × 275 g can crushed pineapple, drained and juice reserved	1 × 10 oz can crushed pineapple, drained and juice reserved
150 ml double or whipping cream	¼ pint double or whipping cream
salt	salt
freshly ground black pepper	freshly ground black pepper
15 g powdered gelatine	½ oz powdered gelatine

Topping:

Metric	Imperial
75 g full fat soft cheese	3 oz full fat soft cheese
2 × 15 ml spoons mayonnaise	2 tablespoons mayonnaise
1 × 15 ml spoon chopped fresh chives	1 tablespoon chopped fresh chives
paprika	paprika

Preparation time: 1 hour 25 minutes (plus chilling)

Melt the butter or margarine in a saucepan over a gentle heat and stir in the biscuit crumbs with the Parmesan cheese and salt and pepper to taste. Press evenly over the bottom of a greased loose-bottomed 18–20 cm/7–8 inch round cake tin. Chill while you make the filling.
Soften the cheese in a large mixing bowl. Beat in the egg yolks, ham, pineapple, cream and salt and pepper to taste. Put the gelatine and 5 × 15 ml spoons/5 tablespoons of the pineapple juice into a small heat-proof bowl over a saucepan of hot water and stir until the gelatine has dissolved. Beat the gelatine into the cheese mixture. Leave to one side until the mixture is on the point of setting.
Whisk the egg whites until stiff and fold lightly but thoroughly into the cheese mixture. Spoon the mixture into the prepared tin and shake the tin gently to level the surface. Chill for 3–4 hours or until set.
Ease the sides of the tin carefully from the cheesecake and lift the set cheesecake out on the tin base. For the topping, soften the cheese in a bowl and beat in the mayonnaise. Spread evenly over the top of the cheesecake. Sprinkle with chopped chives and a little paprika.
Serves 6–8

Smoked haddock cheesecake

Metric
shortcrust pastry made with 100 g plain flour

Imperial
shortcrust pastry made with 4 oz plain flour

Filling:
225 g smoked haddock fillet
grated rind and juice of 1 lemon
150 ml milk
275 g curd or sieved cottage cheese
3 eggs, separated
pinch of grated nutmeg
30 g plain flour
150 ml soured cream
salt
freshly ground black pepper

Filling:
8 oz smoked haddock fillet
grated rind and juice of 1 lemon
¼ pint milk
10 oz curd or sieved cottage cheese
3 eggs, separated
pinch of grated nutmeg
1 oz plain flour
¼ pint soured cream
salt
freshly ground black pepper

Topping:
3 × 15 ml spoons soured cream
2 hard-boiled eggs
2 × 15 ml spoons coarsely chopped fresh parsley

Topping:
3 tablespoons soured cream
2 hard-boiled eggs
2 tablespoons coarsely chopped fresh parsley

Preparation time: 50 minutes
Cooking time: 1½–1¾ hours
Oven: 160°C, 325°F, Gas Mark 3

Roll out the dough and use to line the bottom of a greased loose-bottomed 18–20 cm/7–8 inch round cake tin.

To make the filling, put the smoked haddock into a shallow pan with the lemon juice and milk. Cover the pan and poach the fish gently until it is just tender. Drain the fish and flake, discarding the skin.

Soften the cheese in a large mixing bowl. Beat in the egg yolks, grated nutmeg, lemon rind, flour and soured cream. Stir in the flaked fish with salt and pepper to taste. Whisk the egg whites until stiff and fold lightly but thoroughly into the cheese mixture. Spoon the cheese mixture into the prepared tin and smooth the surface level. Bake in a preheated oven for 1½–1¾ hours or until firm but still spongy to the touch. Spread the top with the soured cream and return to the oven. Continue baking for a few minutes while you prepare the rest of the topping.

Separate the hard-boiled egg yolks from the whites. Push the yolks through a sieve and chop the whites finely. Toss the yolk and white with the parsley.

Ease the sides of the tin carefully away from the cheesecake and lift the hot cooked cheesecake out on the tin base. Sprinkle the top with the egg and parsley mixture. This cheesecake is best served hot, but if you wish to serve it cold, chill it without the egg and parsley topping.
Serves 6–8

Tarama cheesecake

Metric
75 g butter or margarine
175 g water biscuits, finely crushed
1 × 15 ml spoon sesame seeds
salt
freshly ground black pepper

Imperial
3 oz butter or margarine
6 oz water biscuits, finely crushed
1 tablespoon sesame seeds
salt
freshly ground black pepper

Filling:
100 g skinned smoked cod's roe
grated rind and juice of ½ lemon
2 × 15 ml spoons olive oil
225 g full fat soft cheese
2 eggs, separated
1 garlic clove, peeled and crushed
150 ml double or whipping cream
salt
freshly ground black pepper
15 g powdered gelatine
5 × 15 ml spoons water

Filling:
4 oz skinned smoked cod's roe
grated rind and juice of ½ lemon
2 tablespoons olive oil
8 oz full fat soft cheese
2 eggs, separated
1 garlic clove, peeled and crushed
¼ pint double or whipping cream
salt
freshly ground black pepper
½ oz powdered gelatine
5 tablespoons water

Topping:
4 × 15 ml spoons thick mayonnaise
1 × 75 g jar lumpfish roe
lemon butterflies

Topping:
4 tablespoons thick mayonnaise
1 × 3 oz jar lumpfish roe
lemon butterflies

Preparation time: 1¼ hours (plus chilling)

Melt the butter or margarine in a saucepan over a gentle heat and stir in the biscuit crumbs with the sesame seeds and salt and pepper to taste. Press evenly over the bottom of a greased loose-bottomed 18–20/7–8 inch round cake tin. Chill while you make the filling. Beat the cod's roe with the lemon rind and juice and the olive oil. Soften the cheese in a large mixing bowl. Beat in the egg yolks, garlic, cream, cod's roe mixture and salt and pepper to taste. Put the gelatine and water into a small heatproof bowl over a saucepan of hot water and stir until the gelatine has dissolved. Beat the gelatine into the cheese mixture. Leave on one side until the mixture is on the point of setting.

Whisk the egg whites until stiff and fold lightly but thoroughly into the cheese mixture. Spoon the mixture into the prepared tin and shake the tin gently to level the surface. Chill for 3–4 hours or until the filling is set.

Ease the sides of the tin carefully away from the cheesecake and lift the set cheesecake out on the tin base. Spread an even layer of mayonnaise over the top of the cheesecake. Garnish with lumpfish roe and lemon butterflies.
Serves 6–8

Sardine cheesecake

Metric
75 g butter or margarine
175 g water biscuits, finely
   crushed
grated rind of ½ lemon
salt
freshly ground black pepper

Filling:
225 g full fat soft cheese
2 eggs, separated
grated rind and juice of ½
   lemon
1 × 200 g can sardines in
   oil, mashed
150 ml soured cream
2 hard-boiled eggs, finely
   chopped
salt
freshly ground black pepper
15 g powdered gelatine
5 × 15 ml spoons water

Topping:
150 ml soured cream
1 × 175 g can brisling
   (baby sardines), drained
parsley sprigs

Imperial
3 oz butter or margarine
6 oz water biscuits, finely
   crushed
grated rind of ½ lemon
salt
freshly ground black pepper

Filling:
8 oz full fat soft cheese
2 eggs, separated
grated rind and juice of ½
   lemon
1 × 7 oz can sardines in oil,
   mashed
¼ pint soured cream
2 hard-boiled eggs, finely
   chopped
salt
freshly ground black pepper
½ oz powdered gelatine
5 tablespoons water

Topping:
¼ pint soured cream
1 × 6 oz can brisling (baby
   sardines), drained
parsley sprigs

Preparation time: 1¼ hours (plus chilling)

Melt the butter or margarine in a saucepan over a gentle heat and stir in the biscuit crumbs with the lemon rind and salt and pepper to taste. Press evenly over the bottom of a greased loose-bottomed 18–20/7–8 inch round cake tin. Chill while you make the filling. Soften the cheese in a large mixing bowl. Beat in the egg yolks, lemon rind and juice, sardines, soured cream, hard-boiled eggs and salt and pepper to taste. Put the gelatine and water into a small heatproof bowl over a saucepan of hot water and stir until the gelatine has dissolved. Beat the gelatine into the cheese mixture. Leave to one side until the mixture is on the point of setting.
Whisk the egg whites until stiff and fold lightly but thoroughly into the cheese mixture. Spoon the mixture into the prepared tin and shake the tin gently to level the surface. Chill for 3–4 hours or until the filling is set.
Ease the sides of the tin carefully away from the cheesecake and lift the set cheesecake out on the tin base. Spread the soured cream over the top of the cheesecake. Garnish with the brisling and small sprigs of parsley.
Serves 6–8

Sardine cheesecake; Tarama cheesecake; Smoked haddock cheesecake

Creamy cauliflower cheesecake

Metric
shortcrust pastry made with
100 g plain flour

Filling:
1 small cauliflower, or ½
larger one, divided into
florets
grated rind and juice of ½
lemon
salt
275 g curd or sieved cottage
cheese
3 eggs, separated
2 × 15 ml spoons chopped
fresh parsley
30 g plain flour
6 × 15 ml spoons soured
cream
freshly ground black pepper

Topping:
150 ml double or whipping
cream, lightly whipped
3 × 15 ml spoons finely
chopped fresh parsley

Imperial
shortcrust pastry made with
4 oz plain flour

Filling:
1 small cauliflower, or ½
larger one, divided into
florets
grated rind and juice of ½
lemon
salt
10 oz curd or sieved cottage
cheese
3 eggs, separated
2 tablespoons chopped fresh
parsley
1 oz plain flour
6 tablespoons soured
cream
freshly ground black pepper

Topping:
¼ pint double or whipping
cream, lightly whipped
3 tablespoons finely
chopped fresh parsley

Preparation time: 1 hour
Cooking time: 1½–1¾ hours
Oven: 160°C, 325°F, Gas Mark 3

Roll out the dough and use to line the bottom of a greased loose-bottomed 18–20 cm/7–8 inch cake tin. To make the filling; cook the cauliflower in a pan of boiling water with the lemon juice and 1 × 5 ml spoon/ 1 teaspoon salt until tender. Drain the cooked cauliflower thoroughly and mash to a purée.

Soften the cheese in a large mixing bowl. Beat in the egg yolks, grated lemon rind, chopped parsley, flour, soured cream, the mashed cauliflower and salt and pepper to taste. Whisk the egg whites until stiff and fold lightly but thoroughly into the cheese mixture. Spoon the mixture into the prepared tin and smooth the surface level. Bake in a preheated oven for 1½–1¾ hours or until firm but still spongy to the touch.

Ease the sides of the tin carefully away from the cheesecake and lift the hot cooked cheesecake out on the tin base. To serve hot, top the cheesecake with the whipped cream and garnish with criss-cross ribbons of chopped parsley. To serve cold, chill the cooked cheesecake and then top with the cream and parsley garnish.

Serves 6–8

Greek-style cheesecake

Metric
100 g plain flour
pinch of salt
4 × 15 ml spoons water
25 g lard

Imperial
4 oz plain flour
pinch of salt
4 tablespoons water
1 oz lard

Filling:
1 medium aubergine, thinly
  sliced
oil
275 g curd or sieved cottage
  cheese
3 eggs, separated
1 garlic clove, peeled and
  crushed
30 g plain flour
50 g Parmesan cheese,
  grated
salt
freshly ground black pepper
75 g Mozzarella or Bel
  Paese cheese, thinly sliced

Filling:
1 medium aubergine, thinly
  sliced
oil
10 oz curd or sieved cottage
  cheese
3 eggs, separated
1 garlic clove, peeled and
  crushed
1 oz plain flour
2 oz Parmesan cheese,
  grated
salt
freshly ground black pepper
3 oz Mozzarella or Bel
  Paese cheese, thinly sliced

Preparation time: 1 hour
Cooking time: 1 hour 20 minutes
Oven: 160°C, 325°F, Gas Mark 3

Sift the flour and salt into a bowl. Put the water and lard into a saucepan and stir over a gentle heat until melted. Pour onto the flour and mix to a soft smooth dough. Press evenly over the bottom of a greased loose-bottomed 18–20/7–8 inch round cake tin, working the dough up the sides of the tin to a depth of 2.5 cm/1 inch.

To make the filling, arrange the aubergine slices on well-oiled baking sheets and brush the aubergine with a little more oil. Bake in a preheated oven for 15 minutes. Cool.

Soften the cheese in a large mixing bowl. Beat in the egg yolks, garlic, flour, Parmesan cheese and salt and pepper to taste. Whisk the egg whites until stiff and fold lightly but thoroughly into the cheese mixture. Arrange half the aubergine slices in the prepared tin. Spoon in the cheese mixture, smooth the surface level and arrange the remaining aubergine slices on top. Bake in a preheated oven for 1½ hours.

Top the cheesecake with thin slices of Mozzarella or Bel Paese cheese and return to the oven. Bake for a further 15–20 minutes.

Ease the sides of the tin carefully away from the cheesecake and lift the hot cooked cheesecake out on the tin base. This cheesecake is best served hot.
Serves 6–8

Creamy cauliflower cheesecake; Potato cheesecake; Greek-style cheesecake

Potato cheesecake

Metric
100 g plain flour
pinch of salt
4 × 15 ml spoons water
25 g lard

Imperial
4 oz plain flour
pinch of salt
4 tablespoons water
1 oz lard

Filling:
2 medium potatoes, peeled
  and grated
salt
275 g curd or sieved cottage
  cheese
3 eggs, separated
30 g plain flour
25 g Parmesan cheese,
  grated
150 ml soured cream
3 spring onions, finely
  chopped
freshly ground black pepper

Imperial
2 medium potatoes, peeled
  and grated
salt
10 oz curd or sieved cottage
  cheese
3 eggs, separated
1 oz plain flour
1 oz Parmesan cheese,
  grated
¼ pint soured cream
3 spring onions, finely
  chopped
freshly ground black pepper

Topping:
150 ml soured cream
small packet of potato
  crisps, lightly crushed

Topping:
¼ pint soured cream
small packet of potato
  crisps, lightly crushed

Preparation time: 1 hour
Cooking time: 1½–1¾ hours
Oven: 160°C, 325°F, Gas Mark 3

Children will love this cheesecake served with baked beans.

Sift the flour and salt into a bowl. Put the water and lard into a saucepan and stir over a gentle heat until melted. Pour onto the flour and mix to a soft dough. Press evenly over the bottom of a greased loose-bottomed 18–20/7–8 inch round cake tin, working the dough up the sides of the tin to a depth of about 2.5 cm/1 inch.

To make the filling, put the potatoes into a bowl of salted water until needed. Soften the cheese in a large mixing bowl. Beat in the egg yolks, flour, Parmesan cheese, soured cream, spring onions and salt and pepper to taste. Drain the grated potato and squeeze dry in a piece of muslin or thin clean cloth. Stir the potato into the cheese mixture. Whisk the egg whites until stiff and fold lightly but thoroughly into the cheese mixture. Spoon the mixture into the prepared tin and smooth the surface level. Bake in a preheated oven for 1½–1¾ hours or until firm but still spongy to the touch.

Heat the soured cream for the topping gently in a saucepan. Ease the sides of the tin carefully away from the cheesecake and lift the hot cooked cheesecake out on the tin base. Spoon the warm soured cream over the top and sprinkle with the crisps. This cheesecake is best served hot.
Serves 6–8

Bacon and onion cheesecake

Metric
100 g plain flour
pinch of salt
4 × 15 ml spoons water
25 g lard

Imperial
4 oz plain flour
pinch of salt
4 tablespoons water
1 oz lard

Filling:
275 g curd or sieved cottage cheese
3 eggs, separated
30 g plain flour
1 small onion, peeled and grated
100 g cooked bacon, finely chopped or minced
150 ml double or whipping cream
salt
freshly ground black pepper

Filling:
10 oz curd or sieved cottage cheese
3 eggs, separated
1 oz plain flour
1 small onion, peeled and grated
4 oz cooked bacon, finely chopped or minced
¼ pint double or whipping cream
salt
freshly ground black pepper

Topping:
2 tomatoes, sliced
50 g cheese, grated

Topping:
2 tomatoes, sliced
2 oz cheese, grated

Preparation time: 45 minutes
Cooking time: 1¾ hours
Oven: 160°C, 325°F, Gas Mark 3

Sift the flour and salt into a bowl. Put the water and lard into a saucepan and stir over gentle heat until melted. Pour onto the flour and mix to a soft smooth dough. Press evenly over the bottom of a greased loose-bottomed 18–20 cm/7–8 inch round cake tin, working the dough up the sides of the tin to a depth of about 2.5 cm/1 inch.
To make the filling, soften the cheese in a large mixing bowl. Beat in the egg yolks, flour, onion, bacon, cream and salt and pepper to taste. Whisk the egg whites until stiff and fold lightly but thoroughly into the cheese mixture. Spoon the mixture into the prepared tin and smooth the surface level. Bake in a preheated oven for 1½ hours or until firm.
Arrange the tomato slices on top of the cheesecake and sprinkle with the grated cheese. Return to the oven and bake for a further 15 minutes.
Ease the sides of the tin carefully away from the cheesecake and lift the hot cooked cheesecake out on the tin base. Serve immediately.
Serves 6–8

Chicken cheesecake

Metric
75 g butter or margarine
100 g water biscuits, finely crushed
4 × 15 ml spoons dry sage and onion stuffing mix

Imperial
3 oz butter or margarine
4 oz water biscuits, finely crushed
4 tablespoons dry sage and onion stuffing mix

Filling:
275 g curd or sieved cottage cheese
3 eggs, separated
30 g plain flour
175 g cooked chicken meat, finely chopped or minced
2 × 15 ml spoons chopped fresh parsley
150 ml soured cream
salt
freshly ground black pepper

Filling:
10 oz curd or sieved cottage cheese
3 eggs, separated
1 oz plain flour
6 oz cooked chicken meat, finely chopped or minced
2 tablespoons chopped fresh parsley
¼ pint soured cream
salt
freshly ground black pepper

Topping:
25 g butter
1 medium onion, peeled and thinly sliced
150 ml soured cream
2 × 15 ml spoons chopped fresh parsley

Topping:
1 oz butter
1 medium onion, peeled and thinly sliced
¼ pint soured cream
2 tablespoons chopped fresh parsley

Preparation time: 45 minutes
Cooking time: 1½–1¾ hours
Oven: 160°C, 325°F, Gas Mark 3

Melt the butter or margarine in a saucepan over a gentle heat and stir in the biscuit crumbs with the dry stuffing mix. Press over the bottom of a greased loose-bottomed 18–20 cm/7–8 inch round cake tin. Chill.
Soften the cheese in a large mixing bowl. Beat in the egg yolks, flour, chicken, parsley, soured cream and salt and pepper to taste. Whisk the egg whites until stiff and fold lightly but thoroughly into the cheese mixture. Spoon the mixture into the prepared tin and smooth the surface level. Bake in a preheated oven for 1½–1¾ hours or until firm but still spongy to the touch. Just before the cheesecake is ready, make the topping. Melt the butter in a frying pan, add the onion and fry gently until soft and golden. Stir in the soured cream. Ease the sides of the tin carefully away from the cheesecake and lift the hot cooked cheesecake out on the tin base. Spoon the onion-flavoured cream over the top and sprinkle with the chopped parsley.
Serves 6–8

Mushroom rarebit cheesecake

Preparation time: 55 minutes
Cooking time: 1¾ hours
Oven: 160°C, 325°F, Gas Mark 3

Metric
100 g plain flour
pinch of salt
4 × 15 ml spoons water
25 g lard

Filling:
40 g butter
100 g button mushrooms,
  sliced
2 × 15 ml spoons plain flour
150 ml milk
75 g mature Cheddar
  cheese, grated
1 × 5 ml spoon French
  mustard
salt
freshly ground black pepper
275 g curd or sieved cottage
  cheese
3 eggs, separated
4 × 15 ml spoons soured
  cream

Topping:
25 g butter
50 g button mushrooms,
  sliced
50 g mature Cheddar
  cheese, grated
cayenne pepper (optional)

Imperial
4 oz plain flour
pinch of salt
4 tablespoons water
1 oz lard

Filling:
1½ oz butter
4 oz button mushrooms,
  sliced
2 tablespoons plain flour
¼ pint milk
3 oz mature Cheddar
  cheese, grated
1 teaspoon French
  mustard
salt
freshly ground black pepper
10 oz curd or sieved cottage
  cheese
3 eggs, separated
4 tablespoons soured
  cream

Topping:
1 oz butter
2 oz button mushrooms,
  sliced
2 oz mature Cheddar
  cheese, grated
cayenne pepper (optional)

Sift the flour and salt into a bowl. Put the water and lard into a saucepan and stir over gentle heat until melted. Pour into the flour and mix to a soft smooth dough. Press evenly over the bottom of a greased loose-bottomed 18–20 cm/7–8 inch round cake tin, working the dough up the sides of the tin to a depth of 2.5 cm/1 inch.

To make the filling, melt the butter in a saucepan, add the mushrooms and cook for 5–6 minutes or until just tender. Remove the mushrooms with a slotted spoon and keep to one side. Stir the flour into the fat remaining in the pan and cook for 1 minute. Gradually stir in the milk and bring to the boil, stirring until the sauce has thickened. Remove the pan from the heat and beat in the grated cheese, mustard and salt and pepper to taste.

Soften the cheese in a large mixing bowl. Beat in the cheese sauce, egg yolks and soured cream. Whisk the egg whites until stiff and fold lightly but thoroughly into the cheese mixture, together with the cooked mushrooms. Spoon the mixture into the prepared tin and smooth the surface level. Bake in a preheated oven for 1½ hours.

Just before the cheesecake is ready, prepare the topping. Melt the butter in a saucepan, add the mushrooms and fry gently until just tender. Drain the mushrooms and arrange on top of the cooked cheese-cake. Sprinkle with the grated cheese. Return to the oven and bake for a further 15 minutes. Sprinkle with a little cayenne pepper if liked.

Ease the sides of the tin carefully away from the cheesecake and lift the hot cooked cheesecake out on the tin base. Serve warm.
Serves 6–8

Chicken cheesecake; Bacon and onion cheesecake; Mushroom rarebit cheesecake

Avocado cheesecake

Metric
75 g butter or margarine
175 g water biscuits, finely
  crushed
grated rind of ½ lemon
salt
freshly ground black pepper

Filling:
1 large ripe avocado, peeled
  and stoned
grated rind and juice of ½
  lemon
225 g herb-flavoured full
  fat soft cheese
2 eggs, separated
150 ml soured cream
salt
freshly ground black pepper
15 g powdered gelatine
5 × 15 ml spoons water

Topping:
1 small ripe avocado,
  peeled, stoned and thinly
  sliced
juice of 1 lemon
few tarragon sprigs

Imperial
3 oz butter or margarine
6 oz water biscuits, finely
  crushed
grated rind of ½ lemon
salt
freshly ground black pepper

Filling:
1 large ripe avocado, peeled
  and stoned
grated rind and juice of ½
  lemon
8 oz herb-flavoured full fat
  soft cheese
2 eggs, separated
¼ pint soured cream
salt
freshly ground black pepper
½ oz powdered gelatine
5 tablespoons water

Topping:
1 small ripe avocado,
  peeled, stoned and thinly
  sliced
juice of 1 lemon
few tarragon sprigs

Preparation time: 1 hour 25 minutes (plus chilling)

Melt the butter or margarine in a saucepan over a gentle heat and stir in the biscuit crumbs with the lemon rind and salt and pepper to taste. Press evenly over the bottom of a greased loose-bottomed 18–20 cm/7–8 inch round cake tin. Chill while you make the filling.
Mash the avocado flesh with the lemon rind and juice. Soften the herb-flavoured cheese in a large mixing bowl. Beat in the egg yolks, soured cream, mashed avocado and salt and pepper to taste. Put the gelatine and water into a small heatproof bowl over a saucepan of hot water and stir until the gelatine has dissolved. Beat the gelatine into the cheese mixture. Leave to one side until the mixture is on the point of setting.
Whisk the egg whites until stiff and fold lightly but thoroughly into the cheese mixture. Spoon the mixture into the prepared tin and shake the tin gently to level the surface. Chill for 3–4 hours or until the filling is set.
Ease the sides of the tin carefully away from the cheesecake and lift the set cheesecake out on the tin base. For the topping, toss the avocado slices in the lemon juice. Garnish the cheesecake with the slices of avocado and small sprigs of tarragon.
Serves 6–8

Tomato cheesecake

Metric
75 g butter or margarine
175 g digestive biscuits,
  finely crushed
25 g Parmesan cheese,
  grated
salt
freshly ground black pepper

Filling:
225 g full fat soft cheese
1 × 15 ml spoon tomato
  purée
1 × 2.5 ml spoon caster
  sugar
2 eggs, separated
1 small onion, peeled and
  grated
150 ml double or whipping
  cream
1 × 15 ml spoon chopped
  fresh basil
salt
freshly ground black pepper
15 g powdered gelatine
5 × 15 ml spoons water
4 large tomatoes, skinned,
  seeded and chopped

Topping:
2 tomatoes, thinly sliced
few fresh basil leaves

Imperial
3 oz butter or margarine
6 oz digestive biscuits,
  finely crushed
1 oz Parmesan cheese,
  grated
salt
freshly ground black pepper

Filling:
8 oz full fat soft cheese
1 tablespoon tomato
  purée
½ teaspoon caster
  sugar
2 eggs, separated
1 small onion, peeled and
  grated
¼ pint double or whipping
  cream
1 tablespoon chopped fresh
  basil
salt
freshly ground black pepper
½ oz powdered gelatine
5 tablespoons water
4 large tomatoes, skinned,
  seeded and chopped

Topping:
2 tomatoes, thinly sliced
few fresh basil leaves

Preparation time: 1¼ hours (plus chilling)

Melt the butter or margarine in a saucepan over a gentle heat and stir in the biscuit crumbs with the Parmesan cheese and salt and pepper to taste. Press evenly over the bottom of a greased loose-bottomed 18–20 cm/7–8 inch round cake tin. Chill while you make the filling.
Soften the cheese in a large mixing bowl. Beat in the tomato purée, caster sugar, egg yolks, grated onion, cream, basil and salt and pepper to taste. Put the gelatine and water into a small heatproof bowl over a saucepan of hot water and stir until the gelatine has dissolved. Beat the gelatine into the cheese mixture. Leave to one side until the mixture is on the point of setting.
Whisk the egg whites until stiff and fold lightly but thoroughly into the cheese mixture together with the chopped tomato. Spoon the mixture into the prepared tin and shake the tin gently to level the surface. Chill for 3–4 hours or until the filling is set.
Ease the sides of the tin carefully away from the cheesecake and lift the set cheesecake out on the tin base. Garnish with overlapping slices of tomato and a cluster of basil leaves.
Serves 6–8

Minted cucumber cheesecake

Metric
75 g butter or margarine
175 g digestive biscuits,
  finely crushed
grated rind and juice of ½
  lemon
salt
freshly ground black pepper

Filling:
½ large cucumber, peeled
  and coarsely grated
225 g full fat soft cheese
2 eggs, separated
grated rind of ½ lemon
1 × 15 ml spoon mint jelly
150 ml soured cream
1 garlic clove, peeled and
  crushed
salt
freshly ground black pepper
15 g powdered gelatine
5 × 15 ml spoons water

Topping:
150 ml soured cream
1 × 15 ml spoon finely
  chopped fresh mint
few cucumber slices
fresh mint sprigs

Imperial
3 oz butter or margarine
6 oz digestive biscuits,
  finely crushed
grated rind and juice of ½
  lemon
salt
freshly ground black pepper

Filling:
½ large cucumber, peeled
  and coarsely grated
8 oz full fat soft cheese
2 eggs, separated
grated rind of ½ lemon
1 tablespoon mint jelly
¼ pint soured cream
1 garlic clove, peeled and
  crushed
salt
freshly ground black pepper
½ oz powdered gelatine
5 tablespoons water

Topping:
¼ pint soured cream
1 tablespoon finely chopped
  fresh mint
few cucumber slices
fresh mint sprigs

Preparation time: 1 hour 20 minutes (plus chilling)

Melt the butter or margarine in a saucepan over a gentle heat and stir in the biscuit crumbs with the lemon rind and juice and salt and pepper to taste. Press evenly over the bottom of a greased loose-bottomed 18–20 cm/7–8 inch round cake tin. Chill while you make the filling.

Put the grated cucumber into a piece of muslin or a clean thin cloth and squeeze to remove most of the excess moisture. Soften the cheese in a large mixing bowl. Beat in the egg yolks, lemon rind, mint jelly, soured cream, garlic and salt and pepper to taste. Stir in the grated cucumber. Put the gelatine and water into a small heatproof bowl over a saucepan of hot water and stir until the gelatine has dissolved. Beat the gelatine into the cheese mixture. Leave to one side until the mixture is on the point of setting.

Whisk the egg whites until stiff and fold lightly but thoroughly into the cheese mixture. Spoon the mixture into the prepared tin and shake the tin gently to level the surface. Chill for 3–4 hours or until the filling is set.

Ease the sides of the tin carefully away from the cheesecake and lift the set cheesecake out on the tin base. For the topping, mix the soured cream with the chopped mint and spread over the top of the cheesecake. Garnish with cucumber slices and sprigs of mint. Serves 6–8

Avocado cheesecake; Tomato cheesecake; Minted cucumber cheesecake

THE NOT-QUITE CHEESECAKE

Not all cheesecakes come in a regular shape, with a base, filling and topping. Some come in stemmed glasses, some between layers of featherlight pastry, and others in the shape of an ice-cream bombe! These are the not-quite-cheesecakes – based on similar ingredients, but very different in appearance from the traditional cheesecake.

Blushing cheese tarts

Metric	Imperial
shortcrust pastry made with 225 g plain flour	shortcrust pastry made with 8 oz plain flour

Filling:

Metric	Imperial
175 g full fat soft cheese	6 oz full fat soft cheese
100 g caster sugar	4 oz caster sugar
2 eggs, separated	2 eggs, separated
2 × 15 ml spoons redcurrant jelly	2 tablespoons redcurrant jelly
2 × 15 ml spoons double or whipping cream	2 tablespoons double or whipping cream

To decorate:

Metric	Imperial
4 × 15 ml spoons redcurrant jelly	4 tablespoons redcurrant jelly
fresh redcurrants (optional)	fresh redcurrants (optional)

Preparation time: 35 minutes
Cooking time: 25–30 minutes
Oven: 190°C, 375°F, Gas Mark 5

Roll out the pastry quite thinly. Cut into 6 rounds and use to line individual tartlet or patty tins. Prick the bottoms.

To make the filling, soften the cheese in a mixing bowl. Beat in 50g/2oz of the caster sugar, the egg yolks, redcurrant jelly and cream. Whisk the egg whites until stiff, then whisk in the remaining caster sugar. Fold lightly but thoroughly into the cheese mixture. Divide the cheese mixture between the pastry cases. Bake in a preheated oven for 25–30 minutes or until the filling is set. Allow to cool.

For the decoration, put the redcurrant jelly into a saucepan and stir over a gentle heat until the jelly has melted. Spoon over each cheese tart to give an even glaze. Leave until set. Decorate with small sprigs of fresh redcurrants.

Serves 6

Cassata fruit pyramid; Blushing cheese tarts

Cassata fruit pyramid

Metric	Imperial
450 g cottage cheese	1 lb cottage cheese
75 g unsalted butter	3 oz unsalted butter
2 egg yolks	2 egg yolks
75 g caster sugar	3 oz caster sugar
150 ml double or whipping cream	$\frac{1}{4}$ pint double or whipping cream
100 g chopped mixed peel	4 oz chopped mixed peel
50 g blanched almonds, chopped	2 oz blanched almonds, chopped
finely grated rind of $\frac{1}{2}$ orange	finely grated rind of $\frac{1}{2}$ orange

To decorate:

Metric	Imperial
50 g blanched almonds, split and toasted	2 oz blanched almonds, split and toasted
50 g chopped mixed peel	2 oz chopped mixed peel

To serve:

Metric	Imperial
sponge fingers or thin slices of Madeira cake	sponge fingers or thin slices of Madeira cake

Preparation time: 1 hour 20 minutes (plus chilling)

A special pashka mould, which is a tall mould perforated with holes, is available for making this dessert. Alternatively you can use a flower pot with a hole in the base, or a conical sieve.

Put the cottage cheese into a clean piece of muslin or thin cloth and squeeze to remove as much excess moisture from the cheese as possible. Press the cheese through a sieve. Soften the butter in a mixing bowl and beat in the sieved cheese.

Whisk the egg yolks and caster sugar together until thick, light and creamy. Put the cream into a saucepan and bring just to the boil. Stir into the whisked egg yolks and sugar. Return the cream mixture to the saucepan and stir over a gentle heat until the custard thickens. Do not allow the custard to boil or it may curdle. Stand the saucepan of custard in a bowl of iced water and stir until the custard has cooled. Beat the custard into the cheese mixture, together with the chopped peel, almonds and grated orange rind.

Line the pashka mould, flower pot or sieve with a piece of dampened muslin, allowing the muslin to hang over the sides of the mould. Stand the mould in a shallow dish. Pour the cheese mixture into the prepared mould and fold the overhanging muslin lightly over the top. Put a weighted plate on top of the cheese mixture and chill for 6–8 hours, or overnight, or until the cheese mixture is quite firm.

Unwrap the muslin from the top of the mould. Invert a serving plate on top of the mould and carefully turn out the cassata fruit pyramid. Peel off the muslin. Decorate with toasted almonds and chopped peel and serve with sponge fingers or pieces of Madeira cake.

Serves 6–8

Strawberry cheese pie

Preparation time: 30 minutes
Cooking time: 40–45 minutes
Oven: 180°C, 350°F, Gas Mark 4

Metric	Imperial
shortcrust pastry made with 225 g plain flour	shortcrust pastry made with 8 oz plain flour
225 g full fat soft cheese	8 oz full fat soft cheese
100 g caster sugar	4 oz caster sugar
150 ml creamy mayonnaise	¼ pint creamy mayonnaise
2 eggs	2 eggs
grated rind of 1 lemon	grated rind of 1 lemon
few drops of vanilla essence	few drops of vanilla essence

To decorate:

Metric	Imperial
350 g strawberries, hulled	12 oz strawberries, hulled
4 × 15 ml spoons redcurrant jelly	4 tablespoons redcurrant jelly

Roll out the dough and use to line a 20–23 cm/8–9 inch flan tin. Prick the bottom and line with a circle of greaseproof paper. Fill with a layer of baking beans. Bake 'blind' in a preheated oven for 15 minutes. Meanwhile, soften the cheese in a mixing bowl. Beat in the caster sugar, mayonnaise, eggs, lemon rind and vanilla essence. Remove the paper and beans from the pastry case and pour in the cheese mixture. Return to the oven and bake for a further 25–30 minutes or until the filling is just set. Allow to cool.
Arrange the whole or sliced strawberries on top of the cheese pie. Heat the redcurrant jelly in a saucepan over a gentle heat until melted. Spoon the jelly evenly over the strawberries. Chill for 1 hour.
Serves 6–8

Ricotta cheese pudding

Preparation time: 25 minutes
Cooking time: 45 minutes
Oven: 180°C, 350°F, Gas Mark 4

Metric	Imperial
225 g ricotta or sieved cottage cheese	8 oz ricotta or sieved cottage cheese
175 g caster sugar	6 oz caster sugar
2 eggs, separated	2 eggs, separated
100 g plain flour	4 oz plain flour
grated rind of 1 lemon	grated rind of 1 lemon
1 × 5 ml spoon baking powder	1 teaspoon baking powder
75 g seedless raisins	3 oz seedless raisins
50 g blanched almonds, chopped	2 oz blanched almonds, chopped
icing sugar, to serve	icing sugar, to serve

Grease a 20 cm/8 inch shallow cake tin, and line the bottom with a circle of greased greaseproof paper.
Beat the cheese with the caster sugar, egg yolks, flour, lemon rind and baking powder. Whisk the egg whites until stiff and fold lightly but thoroughly into the cheese mixture, together with the raisins and almonds. Spread the mixture evenly in the tin. Bake in a preheated oven for about 45 minutes or until a skewer inserted into the pudding comes out clean. Cool.
Dust the pudding with sifted icing sugar before serving. A fruit purée or compôte of fruits makes a delicious accompaniment.
Serves 6

Coeurs à la crème

Preparation time: 25–30 minutes (plus chilling)

Metric	Imperial
225 g cottage cheese	8 oz cottage cheese
1 × 5 ml spoon salt	1 teaspoon salt
300 ml double or whipping cream	½ pint double or whipping cream

To serve:

Metric	Imperial
300 ml double or whipping cream	½ pint double or whipping cream
berry fruits	berry fruits
granulated sugar	granulated sugar

Small heart-shaped moulds are usually used for making this dessert, but clean empty yogurt cartons, pierced with a few holes, serve the purpose just as well.

Rinse 4–6 moulds or yogurt cartons in cold water; do not dry them. Put the cottage cheese into a clean piece of muslin or thin cloth and squeeze to remove as much excess moisture from the cheese as possible. Put the cheese into a bowl with the salt and work together. Press the cheese through a sieve. Lightly whip the double cream and stir in the sieved cheese.
Spoon the cheese and cream mixture into the moulds or yogurt cartons and stand them on a tray to catch any liquid that drains off. Chill for 6–8 hours.
Unmould the coeurs à la crème on to a serving dish. Spoon a little cream over each one and serve with a bowl of strawberries or raspberries, and sugar.
Serves 4–6

Strawberry cheese pie; Coeurs à la crème; Ricotta cheese pudding

Mon ami

Preparation time: 35–40 minutes

Metric	*Imperial*
2 egg yolks	*2 egg yolks*
50 g caster sugar	*2 oz caster sugar*
100 g full fat soft cheese	*4 oz full fat soft cheese*
2 × 15 ml spoons honey	*2 tablespoons honey*
grated rind and juice of ½ lemon	*grated rind and juice of ½ lemon*
300 ml double or whipping cream	*½ pint double or whipping cream*
angelica leaves, to decorate	*angelica leaves, to decorate*

This is based on a recipe dating from 1542. A bowl of fresh raspberries or strawberries makes a delicious accompaniment.

Put the egg yolks and caster sugar into a heatproof bowl over a saucepan of hot water and whisk until the mixture is thick, light and creamy. Soften the cheese in a mixing bowl and beat in the honey, lemon rind and juice and the whisked egg and sugar mixture. Allow to cool.

Whip the cream until it is thick and fold into the cheese mixture. Spoon into stemmed glasses and chill. Decorate with angelica leaves and serve with sponge fingers or wafers.

Serves 4–6

Truffle cheesecake

Preparation time: 35–40 minutes (plus chilling)

Metric	*Imperial*
175 g plain chocolate	*6 oz plain chocolate*
225 g full fat soft cheese	*8 oz full fat soft cheese*
100 g caster sugar	*4 oz caster sugar*
4 × 15 ml spoons rum	*4 tablespoons rum*
100 g dry sponge cake, crumbled	*4 oz dry sponge cake, crumbled*
75 g walnuts, chopped	*3 oz walnuts, chopped*
100 g glacé cherries, chopped	*4 oz glacé cherries, chopped*
75 g chocolate vermicelli	*3 oz chocolate vermicelli*

To decorate:	*To decorate:*
150 ml double or whipping cream, whipped	*¼ pint double or whipping cream, whipped*
glacé cherries	*glacé cherries*
walnut halves	*walnut halves*

Break the chocolate into small pieces and put into a heatproof bowl over a saucepan of hot water. Stir until the chocolate has melted. Remove from the heat.

Soften the cheese in a mixing bowl. Beat in the caster sugar and rum until the mixture is light and creamy. Stir in the melted chocolate, sponge cake, nuts and cherries. If the mixture seems too soft to handle, chill for 30 minutes before moulding. Either press into a log shape mould, or roll into a sausage shape like a small Swiss roll. Coat the shaped mixture evenly with the chocolate vermicelli. Chill for 1 hour.

Pipe the truffle cheesecake with whipped cream and decorate with glacé cherries and walnuts.

Serves 6

Crostata

Preparation time: 35 minutes
Cooking time: 1 hour
Oven: 180°C, 350°F, Gas Mark 4

Metric	*Imperial*
rich shortcrust pastry made with 350 g plain flour	*rich shortcrust pastry made with 12 oz plain flour*
750 g ricotta or sieved cottage cheese	*1½ lb ricotta or sieved cottage cheese*
100 g caster sugar	*4 oz caster sugar*
1 × 15 ml spoon plain flour	*1 tablespoon plain flour*
1 × 5 ml spoon salt	*1 teaspoon salt*
few drops of vanilla essence	*few drops of vanilla essence*
finely grated rind of 1 orange	*finely grated rind of 1 orange*
1 egg, separated	*1 egg, separated*
2 egg yolks	*2 egg yolks*
75 g sultanas	*3 oz sultanas*
75 g chopped mixed peel	*3 oz chopped mixed peel*
50 g pine kernels or strip almonds	*2 oz pine kernels or strip almonds*

Roll out two-thirds of the dough and use to line a greased loose-bottomed 20–23 cm/8–9 inch flan tin.

Mix the cheese with the caster sugar, flour, salt, vanilla essence, grated orange rind, 3 egg yolks, sultanas and mixed peel. Spread the cheese mixture evenly in the pastry case.

Roll out the remaining dough and cut into strips about 1 cm/½ inch wide. Criss-cross the strips over the cheese filling to give a lattice effect and pinch the ends of the strips to the edge of the pastry case. Whisk the egg white lightly and brush over the dough lattice. Sprinkle with the pine kernels or almonds.

Bake in a preheated oven for 1 hour or until the pastry is golden and the cheese filling firm. Allow to cool before unmoulding the crostata.

Serves 6–8

Cream cheese mille feuilles

Metric
*puff pastry made with
  225 g plain flour or 375 g
  frozen puff pastry,
  thawed
1 egg white
caster sugar*

Imperial
*puff pastry made with 8 oz
  plain flour or 13 oz
  frozen puff pastry,
  thawed
1 egg white
caster sugar*

Filling:
*175 g full fat soft cheese
75 g caster sugar
150 ml double cream
3 × 15 ml spoons raspberry
  jam*

Filling:
*6 oz full fat soft cheese
3 oz caster sugar
¼ pint double cream
3 tablespoons raspberry
  jam*

Topping:
*100 g icing sugar, sifted
50 g plain chocolate*

Topping:
*4 oz icing sugar, sifted
2 oz plain chocolate*

Top shelf: Mon ami; Cream cheese mille feuilles. Bottom shelf: Truffle cheesecake; Crostata

Preparation time: 40 minutes
Cooking time: 20 minutes
Oven: 200°C, 400°F, Gas Mark 6

Roll out the pastry quite thinly and cut into two strips, each 20 by 7.5 cm/8 by 3 inches. Place on greased baking sheets and prick at regular intervals. Whisk the egg white lightly and brush over the dough strips. Sprinkle with caster sugar and leave to rest for 30 minutes. Bake in a preheated oven for about 20 minutes or until lightly golden and well risen. Allow to cool.

Soften the cheese in a mixing bowl. Beat in the caster sugar. Lightly whip the cream and fold into the cheese mixture. Spread one baked pastry strip with the raspberry jam and top with the cream cheese mixture. Place the second pastry strip on top.

Mix the icing sugar with a little hot water to give a thin coating icing. Melt the chocolate in a heatproof bowl over a saucepan of hot water. Spread the icing evenly over the mille feuilles and pipe thin parallel lines of chocolate on the icing. Drag at regular intervals with the tip of a knife to give a feathered effect. Allow to set.

Serves 6–8

Frozen lemon cheesecake

Preparation time: 25 minutes (plus freezing)

Metric
225 g full fat soft cheese
100 g caster sugar
grated rind and juice of 2
  lemons
2 egg yolks
300 ml double or whipping
  cream

Imperial
8 oz full fat soft cheese
4 oz caster sugar
grated rind and juice of 2
  lemons
2 egg yolks
½ pint double or whipping
  cream

To decorate:
small mint leaves
whisked egg white
caster sugar

To decorate:
small mint leaves
whisked egg white
caster sugar

Soften the cheese in a mixing bowl. Beat in the caster sugar, lemon rind and juice and the egg yolks. Whip the cream until it is thick and fold into the cheese mixture. Spoon into a dampened metal 'bombe' mould, or a freezerproof jelly mould. Put into the freezer and freeze until quite firm and icy.

Meanwhile, prepare the decoration. Dip the mint leaves into whisked egg white, then dust evenly with caster sugar. Allow to dry at room temperature.

Carefully unmould the frozen lemon cheesecake on to a serving dish and decorate with the frosted mint leaves. Serve immediately.

Serves 4–6

Blackberry cheese shortcake

Metric
225 g plain flour
50 g icing sugar
175 g butter, softened
1 egg yolk
2 × 15 ml spoons double or
  whipping cream

Filling:
175 g full fat soft cheese
100 g caster sugar
1 egg white
150 ml double or whipping
  cream
225 g fresh blackberries
icing sugar

Imperial
8 oz plain flour
2 oz icing sugar
6 oz butter, softened
1 egg yolk
2 tablespoons double or
  whipping cream

Filling:
6 oz full fat soft cheese
4 oz caster sugar
1 egg white
¼ pint double or whipping
  cream
8 oz fresh blackberries
icing sugar

Preparation time: 1 hour 20 minutes
Cooking time: 12–15 minutes
Oven: 190°C, 375°F, Gas Mark 5

Sift the flour and icing sugar into a bowl. Add the butter cut into small pieces, and the egg yolk mixed with the cream. Work to a soft smooth dough. Divide the dough into two equal portions. Roll out each portion to a 20–23 cm/8–9 inch round and place on two greased baking sheets. Mark the top of one shortcake round into 8 sections, without cutting right through. Chill for 30 minutes.

Bake the shortcakes in a preheated oven for 12–15 minutes or until lightly golden. Cut through the marked divisions on the one shortcake round and leave to cool on the baking sheets.

To make the filling, soften the cheese in a mixing bowl and beat in the caster sugar. Whisk the egg white until stiff. Whip the cream. Fold the egg white into the whipped cream, then fold the lightened cream into the cheese mixture with most of the blackberries.

Put the uncut shortcake round onto a plate and top with the blackberry cream, mounding it up in the centre. Arrange the sections of shortcake on top, so that they come to a point in the centre. Decorate with the reserved blackberries and dust lightly with sifted icing sugar.
Serves 6–8

Raspberry cheese charlotte

Metric
20–24 sponge fingers
sherry
225 g raspberries
juice of 1 orange
75 g caster sugar
225 g full fat soft cheese
3 eggs, separated
2 × 15 ml spoons brandy
20 g powdered gelatine
5 × 15 ml spoons water
300 ml double or whipping
  cream

To decorate:
150 ml double or whipping
  cream, whipped
raspberries

Imperial
20–24 sponge fingers
sherry
8 oz raspberries
juice of 1 orange
3 oz caster sugar
8 oz full fat soft cheese
3 eggs, separated
2 tablespoons brandy
¾ oz powdered gelatine
5 tablespoons water
½ pint double or whipping
  cream

To decorate:
¼ pint double or whipping
  cream, whipped
raspberries

Preparation time: 1 hour 5 minutes (plus chilling)

Trim one end of each sponge finger so that it has a flat base. Moisten the sponge fingers with a little sherry and use to line the sides of a lightly greased loose-bottomed 18–20 cm/7–8 inch round cake tin. The sponge fingers standing upright, sugar side against the tin, should touch so that the sides of the tin are completely lined.

Put the raspberries into the blender goblet with the orange juice and sugar and blend until smooth. Soften the cheese in a mixing bowl. Beat in the egg yolks, brandy and the raspberry purée. Put the gelatine and water into a small heatproof bowl over a saucepan of hot water and stir until the gelatine has dissolved. Stir the gelatine into the cheese and raspberry mixture. Leave on one side until the mixture is on the point of setting.

Lightly whip the cream. Whisk the egg whites until stiff. Fold the cream and egg whites lightly but thoroughly into the cheese mixture. Spoon into the sponge-lined tin. Chill for 3–4 hours or until the filling is set.

Carefully ease the sides of the tin away from the charlotte and lift the set charlotte out on the tin base. Decorate with piped cream and raspberries.
Serves 6

Blackberry cheese shortcake; Frozen lemon cheesecake;
Raspberry cheese charlotte

PARTY CHEESECAKES

It is at a party that a cheesecake really comes into its own – it looks impressive, and is easy to eat with a fork. The other sections in this book have dealt with cheesecakes for everyday eating. The cheesecakes in this section, however, are rather special. The sweet cheesecakes are luscious and extravagant-looking, and the savoury ones are rich with such delicacies as crab and prawns. Because they are rich, only a small amount is needed for each person.

Fresh salmon cheesecake;
Smoked salmon cheesecake

Fresh salmon cheesecake

Metric	Imperial
100 g butter or margarine	4 oz butter or margarine
175 g water biscuits, finely crushed	6 oz water biscuits, finely crushed
grated rind of 1 lemon	grated rind of 1 lemon
salt	salt
freshly ground black pepper	freshly ground black pepper

Filling:

Metric	Imperial
450 g full fat soft cheese	1 lb full fat soft cheese
grated rind and juice of 1 lemon	grated rind and juice of 1 lemon
4 eggs, separated	4 eggs, separated
about 225 g cooked fresh or canned salmon, flaked	about 8 oz cooked fresh or canned salmon, flaked
½ medium cucumber, peeled and coarsely grated	½ medium cucumber, peeled and coarsely grated
300 ml double or whipping cream	½ pint double or whipping cream
4 × 15 ml spoons mayonnaise	4 tablespoons mayonnaise
salt	salt
freshly ground black pepper	freshly ground black pepper
40 g powdered gelatine	1½ oz powdered gelatine
8 × 15 ml spoons water	8 tablespoons water

Topping:

Metric	Imperial
6 × 15 ml spoons thick mayonnaise	6 tablespoons thick mayonnaise
thin lemon slices	thin lemon slices
cucumber slices	cucumber slices
paprika	paprika

Preparation time: 1 hour 20 minutes (plus chilling)

Melt the butter or margarine in a saucepan over a gentle heat and stir in the water biscuit crumbs with the lemon rind and salt and pepper to taste. Press evenly over the bottom of a greased loose-bottomed 25–30 cm/10–12 inch round cake tin. Chill while you make the filling.

Soften the cheese in a large mixing bowl. Beat in the lemon rind and juice, egg yolks, flaked salmon, grated cucumber, cream, mayonnaise and salt and pepper to taste. Put the gelatine and water into a small heatproof bowl over a saucepan of hot water and stir until the gelatine has dissolved. Beat the gelatine into the cheese mixture. Leave on one side until the mixture is on the point of setting.

Whisk the egg whites until stiff and fold lightly but thoroughly into the cheese mixture. Spoon the mixture into the prepared tin and shake the tin gently to level the surface. Chill for 3–4 hours or until set.

Ease the sides of the tin carefully away from the cheesecake and lift the set cheesecake out on the tin base. Spread the mayonnaise evenly over the top of the cheesecake. Garnish with thin lemon and cucumber slices and sprinkle with paprika.

Serves 10–12

Smoked salmon cheesecake

Metric	Imperial
100 g butter or margarine	4 oz butter or margarine
175 g water biscuits, finely crushed	6 oz water biscuits, finely crushed
3 × 15 ml spoons chopped fresh parsley	3 tablespoons chopped fresh parsley
salt	salt
freshly ground black pepper	freshly ground black pepper

Filling:

Metric	Imperial
450 g full fat soft cheese	1 lb full fat soft cheese
grated rind and juice of 1 lemon	grated rind and juice of 1 lemon
4 eggs, separated	4 eggs, separated
1 × 15 ml spoon tomato purée	1 tablespoon tomato purée
300 ml soured cream	½ pint soured cream
salt	salt
freshly ground black pepper	freshly ground black pepper
30 g powdered gelatine	1 oz powdered gelatine
8 × 15 ml spoons water	8 tablespoons water
175 g smoked salmon trimmings, chopped	6 oz smoked salmon trimmings, chopped
75 g stuffed olives, halved	3 oz stuffed olives, halved

Topping:

Metric	Imperial
3 × 15 ml spoons thick mayonnaise	3 tablespoons thick mayonnaise
4 × 15 ml spoons chopped fresh parsley	4 tablespoons chopped fresh parsley
175 g full fat soft cheese	6 oz full fat soft cheese
juice of ½ lemon	juice of ½ lemon
8 stuffed olives, sliced	8 stuffed olives, sliced

Preparation time: 1 hour (plus chilling)

Melt the butter or margarine in a saucepan over a gentle heat and stir in the water biscuit crumbs with the parsley and salt and pepper to taste. Press evenly over the bottom of a greased loose-bottomed 25–30 cm/10–12 inch round cake tin. Chill.

Soften the cheese in a large mixing bowl. Beat in the lemon rind and juice, egg yolks, tomato purée, soured cream and salt and pepper to taste. Put the gelatine and water into a small heatproof bowl over a saucepan of hot water and stir until the gelatine has dissolved. Beat the gelatine into the cheese mixture. Leave on one side until the mixture is on the point of setting.

Whisk the egg whites until stiff and fold lightly but thoroughly into the cheese mixture, together with the chopped smoked salmon and the stuffed olives. Spoon the mixture into the tin, chill for 3–4 hours.

Ease the sides of the tin carefully away from the cheesecake and lift the set cheesecake out on the tin base. Spread the side of the cheesecake evenly with the mayonnaise and coat with the chopped parsley. Beat the cheese with the lemon juice until soft, and pipe on the cheesecake. Garnish with sliced stuffed olives.

Serves 10–12

Green summer cheesecake

Green summer cheesecake; Layered salad cheesecake; Blue cheese cheesecake

Metric
100 g butter or margarine
175 g water biscuits, finely
  crushed
2 × 15 ml spoons chopped
  fresh parsley
salt
freshly ground black pepper

Filling:
450 g full fat soft cheese
4 eggs, separated
1 garlic clove, peeled and
  crushed
salt
freshly ground black pepper
300 ml double or whipping
  cream
1 × 15 ml spoon chopped
  fresh tarragon
1 × 15 ml spoon chopped
  fresh basil
1 bunch watercress
4 spring onions, chopped
30 g powdered gelatine
8 × 15 ml spoons water
6 × 15 ml spoons chopped
  fresh parsley

Topping:
8 spring onions
175 g full fat soft cheese
3 × 15 ml spoons thick
  mayonnaise
small watercress sprigs

Imperial
4 oz butter or margarine
6 oz water biscuits, finely
  crushed
2 tablespoons chopped fresh
  parsley
salt
freshly ground black pepper

Filling:
1 lb full fat soft cheese
4 eggs, separated
1 garlic clove, peeled and
  crushed
salt
freshly ground black pepper
½ pint double or whipping
  cream
1 tablespoon chopped fresh
  tarragon
1 tablespoon chopped fresh
  basil
1 bunch watercress
4 spring onions, chopped
1 oz powdered gelatine
8 tablespoons water
6 tablespoons chopped fresh
  parsley

Topping:
8 spring onions
6 oz full fat soft cheese
3 tablespoons thick
  mayonnaise
small watercress sprigs

Preparation time: 1½ hours (plus chilling)

Melt the butter or margarine in a saucepan over a gentle heat and stir in the water biscuit crumbs with the parsley and salt and pepper to taste. Press evenly over the bottom of a greased loose-bottomed 25–30 cm/10–12 inch round cake tin. Chill while you make the filling.

Soften the cheese in a large mixing bowl. Beat in the egg yolks, garlic and salt and pepper to taste. Put the cream into the blender goblet with the tarragon, basil and watercress leaves and blend until smooth. Beat the herbed cream into the cheese mixture, together with the chopped spring onions. Put the gelatine and water into a small heatproof bowl over a saucepan of hot water and stir until the gelatine has dissolved. Beat the gelatine into the cheese mixture. Leave on one side until the mixture is on the point of setting.

Whisk the egg whites until stiff and fold lightly but thoroughly into the cheese mixture. Spoon half the cheese mixture into the prepared tin and shake the tin gently to level the surface. Sprinkle over the chopped parsley, then top with the remaining cheese mixture and smooth the surface. Chill for 3–4 hours or until the filling is set.

Meanwhile make spring onion 'water lilies' for the garnish: trim the bulb end of each spring onion so that it is about 6 cm/2½ inches long. Using a sharp knife or kitchen scissors, cut down the spring onion at regular intervals to within 2 cm/¾ inch of the base. Put the onions into a bowl of iced water and leave on one side until the onion 'water lilies' open out.

Ease the sides of the tin carefully away from the cheesecake and lift the set cheesecake out on the tin base. For the topping, soften the cheese and beat in the mayonnaise. Pipe the cheese mixture decoratively on top of the cheesecake. Garnish with the spring onion water lilies and small sprigs of watercress.
Serves 10–12

Layered salad cheesecake

Metric	Imperial
100 g butter or margarine	4 oz butter or margarine
175 g water biscuits, finely crushed	6 oz water biscuits, finely crushed
50 g Parmesan cheese, grated	2 oz Parmesan cheese, grated
salt	salt
freshly ground black pepper	freshly ground black pepper

Filling:	Filling:
450 g full fat soft cheese	1 lb full fat soft cheese
4 eggs, separated	4 eggs, separated
75 g Parmesan cheese, grated	3 oz Parmesan cheese, grated
150 ml double or whipping cream	¼ pint double or whipping cream
150 ml mayonnaise	¼ pint mayonnaise
salt	salt
freshly ground black pepper	freshly ground black pepper
30 g powdered gelatine	1 oz powdered gelatine
8 × 15 ml spoons water	8 tablespoons water
1 large red pepper, cored, seeded and cut into thin strips or finely chopped	1 large red pepper, cored, seeded and cut into thin strips or finely chopped
⅓ large cucumber, thinly sliced	⅓ large cucumber, thinly sliced
100 g sliced salami, cut into strips	4 oz sliced salami, cut into strips

Preparation time: 1¾ hours (plus chilling)

Melt the butter or margarine in a saucepan over a gentle heat and stir in the water biscuit crumbs with the cheese and salt and pepper to taste. Press evenly over the bottom of a greased loose-bottomed 25–30 cm/10–12 inch round cake tin. Chill while you make the filling.

Soften the cheese in a large mixing bowl. Beat in the egg yolks, Parmesan cheese, cream, mayonnaise and salt and pepper to taste. Put the gelatine and water into a small heatproof bowl over a saucepan of hot water and stir until the gelatine has dissolved. Beat the gelatine into the cheese mixture. Leave on one side until the mixture is on the point of setting.

Whisk the egg whites until stiff and fold lightly but thoroughly into the cheese mixture. Spoon one-quarter of the cheese mixture into the prepared tin and smooth it level. Top with the red pepper. Add another quarter of the cheese mixture in a thin even layer, and top with the sliced cucumber. Add a further quarter of the cheese mixture and top with the strips of salami. Finally add the remaining cheese mixture in a thin even layer. Chill for 3–4 hours or until the filling is set. Ease the sides of the tin carefully away from the cheesecake and lift the set cheesecake out on the tin base. If you wish to decorate the cheesecake, top with cornets of salami filled with more cheese, and curls of spring onion.
Serves 10–12

Blue cheese cheesecake

Metric	Imperial
100 g butter or margarine	4 oz butter or margarine
175 g water biscuits, finely crushed	6 oz water biscuits, finely crushed
2 × 15 ml spoons poppy seeds	2 tablespoons poppy seeds
garlic salt	garlic salt
freshly ground black pepper	freshly ground black pepper

Filling:	Filling:
275 g full fat soft cheese	10 oz full fat soft cheese
175 g Danish blue cheese, or other blue cheese, crumbled	6 oz Danish blue cheese, or other blue cheese, crumbled
4 eggs, separated	4 eggs, separated
1 × 5 ml spoon French mustard	1 teaspoon French mustard
300 ml double or whipping cream	½ pint double or whipping cream
garlic salt	garlic salt
freshly ground black pepper	freshly ground black pepper
30 g powdered gelatine	1 oz powdered gelatine
8 × 15 ml spoons water	8 tablespoons water
100 g walnuts, chopped	4 oz walnuts, chopped

Topping:	Topping:
paprika	paprika
12 walnut halves	12 walnut halves
100 g full fat soft cheese	4 oz full fat soft cheese
small cluster of black grapes	small cluster of black grapes

Preparation time: 1½ hours (plus chilling)

Melt the butter or margarine in a saucepan over a gentle heat and stir in the water biscuit crumbs together with the poppy seeds, and garlic salt and pepper to taste. Press evenly over the bottom of a greased loose-bottomed 25–30 cm/10–12 inch round cake tin. Chill while you make the filling.

Soften the full fat cheese in a large mixing bowl. Beat in the blue cheese until smooth. Beat in the egg yolks, mustard, cream, and garlic salt and pepper to taste. Put the gelatine and water into a small heatproof bowl over a saucepan of hot water and stir until the gelatine has dissolved. Beat the gelatine into the cheese mixture. Leave until on the point of setting.

Whisk the egg whites until stiff. Fold lightly but thoroughly into the cheese mixture, together with the chopped walnuts. Spoon the mixture into the prepared tin and shake the tin gently to level the surface. Chill for 3–4 hours or until the filling is set.

Ease the sides of the tin carefully away from the cheesecake and lift the set cheesecake out on the tin base. Sprinkle paprika on top and decorate with walnut halves sandwiched with the cheese, and black grapes.
Serves 10–12

Seafood cheesecake

Metric	Imperial
100 g butter or margarine	4 oz butter or margarine
175 g water biscuits, finely crushed	6 oz water biscuits, finely crushed
1 × 5 ml spoon anchovy essence	1 teaspoon anchovy essence
salt	salt
freshly ground black pepper	freshly ground black pepper

Filling:	**Filling:**
450 g full fat soft cheese	1 lb full fat soft cheese
grated rind and juice of ½ lemon	grated rind and juice of ½ lemon
4 eggs, separated	4 eggs, separated
300 ml double or whipping cream	½ pint double or whipping cream
1 × 15 ml spoon anchovy essence	1 tablespoon anchovy essence
salt	salt
freshly ground black pepper	freshly ground black pepper
30 g powdered gelatine	1 oz powdered gelatine
8 × 15 ml spoons dry white wine	8 tablespoons dry white wine

Topping:	**Topping:**
300 ml soured cream	½ pint soured cream
150 ml mayonnaise	¼ pint mayonnaise
1 garlic clove, peeled and crushed	1 garlic clove, peeled and crushed
salt	salt
freshly ground black pepper	freshly ground black pepper
75 g peeled prawns	3 oz peeled prawns
100 g shelled mussels	4 oz shelled mussels
4 scallops, cooked and chopped	4 scallops, cooked and chopped
100 g cooked white crabmeat, or lobster, flaked	4 oz cooked white crabmeat, or lobster, flaked
8 anchovy fillets	8 anchovy fillets
few cooked mussels or prawns in their shells (optional)	few cooked mussels or prawns in their shells (optional)
parsley sprigs	parsley sprigs

Above: Crab cheesecake; Cocktail cheesecake; Seafood cheesecake

Preparation time: 1 hour 25 minutes (plus chilling)

First make the filling: soften the cheese in a large mixing bowl. Beat in the lemon rind and juice, egg yolks, cream, anchovy essence and salt and pepper to taste. Put the gelatine and white wine into a small heatproof bowl over a saucepan of hot water and stir until the gelatine has dissolved. Beat the gelatine into the cheese mixture. Leave on one side until the mixture is on the point of setting.

Whisk the egg whites until stiff and fold lightly but thoroughly into the cheese mixture. Spoon the mixture into a greased deep 25 cm/10 inch ring mould and shake the mould gently to level the surface.

Melt the butter or margarine in a saucepan over a gentle heat and stir in the water biscuit crumbs with the anchovy essence and salt and pepper to taste. Sprinkle evenly over the cheesecake filling and press the biscuit mixture down very gently. Chill for 3–4 hours or until the filling is set.

Ease the sides of the mould carefully away from the cheesecake and invert the set cheesecake onto a plate. For the topping, mix together the soured cream, mayonnaise, garlic and salt and pepper to taste. Stir in the prawns, mussels, scallops and crabmeat or lobster. Spoon into the centre of the cheesecake ring, allowing a little of the seafood filling to trickle down the sides. Garnish with anchovy fillets, mussels or prawns in their shells, and small sprigs of parsley.
Serves 10–12

Crab cheesecake

Metric	Imperial
100 g butter or margarine	4 oz butter or margarine
175 g water biscuits, finely crushed	6 oz water biscuits, finely crushed
1 × 15 ml spoon fennel seed	1 tablespoon fennel seed
grated rind of ½ lemon	grated rind of ½ lemon
salt	salt
freshly ground black pepper	freshly ground black pepper

Filling:

Metric	Imperial
450 g full fat soft cheese	1 lb full fat soft cheese
grated rind and juice of 1 lemon	grated rind and juice of 1 lemon
4 eggs, separated	4 eggs, separated
300 ml double or whipping cream	½ pint double or whipping cream
salt	salt
freshly ground black pepper	freshly ground black pepper
30 g powdered gelatine	1 oz powdered gelatine
6 × 15 ml spoons dry white wine	6 tablespoons dry white wine
225 g cooked white crabmeat, flaked	8 oz cooked white crabmeat, flaked
50 g peeled prawns, chopped	2 oz peeled prawns, chopped

Topping:

Metric	Imperial
300 ml soured cream	½ pint soured cream
100 g peeled prawns, chopped	4 oz peeled prawns, chopped
75 g black lumpfish roe	3 oz black lumpfish roe
12 unpeeled prawns	12 unpeeled prawns

Preparation time: 1 hour 25 minutes (plus chilling)

Melt the butter or margarine in a saucepan over a gentle heat and stir in the water biscuit crumbs with the fennel seed, lemon rind and salt and pepper to taste. Press evenly over the bottom of a greased loose-bottomed 25–30 cm/10–12 inch round cake tin. Chill. Soften the cheese in a large mixing bowl. Beat in the lemon rind and juice, egg yolks, cream and salt and pepper to taste. Put the gelatine and white wine into a small heatproof bowl over a saucepan of hot water and stir until the gelatine has dissolved. Beat the gelatine into the cheese mixture. Leave on one side until the mixture is on the point of setting.
Whisk the egg whites until stiff and fold lightly but thoroughly into the cheese mixture, together with the flaked crabmeat and chopped prawns. Spoon the mixture into the prepared tin and shake the tin gently to level the surface. Chill for 3–4 hours until set.
Ease the sides of the tin carefully away from the cheesecake and lift the set cheesecake out on the tin base. Mix the soured cream with the chopped prawns and spread over the top of the cheesecake. Garnish with small spoons of lumpfish roe and prawns.
Serves 10–12

Cocktail cheesecake

Metric	Imperial
450 g full fat soft cheese	1 lb full fat soft cheese
4 eggs, separated	4 eggs, separated
200 ml double or whipping cream	⅓ pint double or whipping cream
175 g cooked ham, finely chopped or minced	6 oz cooked ham, finely chopped or minced
salt	salt
freshly ground black pepper	freshly ground black pepper
40 g powdered gelatine	1½ oz powdered gelatine
8 × 15 ml spoons water	8 tablespoons water
toasted fine breadcrumbs or chopped parsley or finely chopped toasted nuts	toasted fine breadcrumbs or chopped parsley or finely chopped toasted nuts

Preparation time: 1 hour 10 minutes (plus chilling)

These cocktail cheesecakes should be served like canapés, as an accompaniment to drinks. The mixture is slightly firmer than that used for an ordinary chilled cheesecake, so that it can be unmoulded, rolled in a coating, and served cut into thin slices. The filling given above is a basic one and can be varied according to taste: you can use chopped cooked chicken, flaked cooked fish, chopped prawns, grated cheese, etc. For moulding the cocktail cheesecakes, you can use any smooth, straight-sided, narrow metal moulds or tumblers. The quantities given in this recipe are sufficient for about 5 good-size tumblers.

Grease the moulds. Soften the cheese in a large mixing bowl. Beat in the egg yolks, cream, ham (or other chosen ingredient) and salt and pepper to taste. Put the gelatine and water into a small heatproof bowl over a saucepan of hot water and stir until the gelatine has dissolved. Beat the gelatine into the cheese mixture. Leave on one side until the mixture is on the point of setting.
Whisk the egg whites until stiff and fold lightly but thoroughly into the cheese mixture. Spoon the mixture into the prepared moulds and shake them gently to level the surface. Chill for 3–4 hours or until set.
Wrap a cloth wrung out in hot water around each mould to loosen the set cheesecakes. Carefully unmould the cheesecakes onto a greased surface. Roll in toasted breadcrumbs, chopped parsley or toasted nuts to give an even coating. Chill for a further 30 minutes. Cut into thin slices to serve.
Serves 24–30

Redcurrant cheesecake

Metric
2 small jam-filled Swiss rolls, cut into 1 cm thick slices

Filling:
450 g full fat soft cheese
4 × 15 ml spoons redcurrant jelly, melted
225 g caster sugar
4 eggs, separated
300 ml double or whipping cream
30 g powdered gelatine
6 × 15 ml spoons water
225 g raspberries, washed and dried

Topping:
300 ml double or whipping cream
2 × 15 ml spoons Cointreau
225 g raspberries, washed and dried
100 g redcurrants, washed and dried

Imperial
2 small jam-filled Swiss rolls, cut into ½ inch thick slices

Filling:
1 lb full fat soft cheese
4 tablespoons redcurrant jelly, melted
8 oz caster sugar
4 eggs, separated
½ pint double or whipping cream
1 oz powdered gelatine
6 tablespoons water
8 oz raspberries, washed and dried

Topping:
½ pint double or whipping cream
2 tablespoons Cointreau
8 oz raspberries, washed and dried
4 oz redcurrants, washed and dried

Preparation time: 1¼ hours (plus chilling)

Arrange the Swiss roll slices in the bottom of a greased loose-bottomed 25–30 cm/10–12 inch round cake tin, pressing them gently together so that they completely cover the bottom of the tin.

To make the filling, soften the cheese in a large mixing bowl. Beat in the redcurrant jelly, 100 g/4 oz of the sugar, the egg yolks and cream. Put the gelatine and water into a small heatproof bowl over a saucepan of hot water and stir until the gelatine has dissolved. Beat the gelatine into the cheese mixture. Leave on one side until the mixture is on the point of setting.

Whisk the egg whites until stiff, then whisk in the remaining sugar. Fold lightly but thoroughly into the cheese mixture, together with the raspberries. Spoon the mixture into the prepared tin and shake the tin gently to level the surface. Chill for 3–4 hours or until the filling is set.

Ease the sides of the tin carefully away from the cheesecake and lift the set cheesecake out on the tin base. For the topping, whip the cream with the Cointreau until thick. Pipe or swirl on top of the cheesecake. Decorate with the raspberries and redcurrants.

Serves 10–12

Grape cheesecake

Metric	Imperial
1 thin sponge layer, 25–30 cm in diameter and 1 cm thick	1 thin sponge layer, 10–12 inches in diameter and ½ inch thick

Filling:

450 g full fat soft cheese	1 lb full fat soft cheese
4 eggs, separated	4 eggs, separated
225 g caster sugar	8 oz caster sugar
grated rind and juice of ½ lemon	grated rind and juice of ½ lemon
6 × 15 ml spoons sweet white vermouth	6 tablespoons sweet white vermouth
300 ml double or whipping cream	½ pint double or whipping cream
30 g powdered gelatine	1 oz powdered gelatine
6 × 15 ml spoons water	6 tablespoons water
175 g seedless green grapes, skinned and halved	6 oz seedless green grapes, skinned and halved

Topping:

small clusters of grapes	small clusters of grapes
2 egg whites, lightly whisked	2 egg whites, lightly whisked
caster sugar	caster sugar
300 ml double or whipping cream, whipped	½ pint double or whipping cream, whipped

Preparation time: 1 hour 20 minutes (plus chilling)

Press the sponge layer into a greased loose-bottomed 25–30 cm/10–12 inch round cake tin, trimming the cake to fit exactly into the bottom of the tin.

To make the filling, soften the cheese in a large mixing bowl. Beat in the egg yolks, 100 g/4 oz of the sugar, lemon rind and juice, vermouth and cream. Put the gelatine and water into a small heatproof bowl over a saucepan of hot water and stir until the gelatine has dissolved. Beat the gelatine into the cheese mixture. Leave to one side until the mixture is on the point of setting.

Whisk the egg whites until stiff, then whisk in the remaining sugar. Fold lightly but thoroughly into the cheese mixture, together with the halved and skinned grapes. Spoon the mixture into the prepared tin and shake the tin gently to level the surface. Chill for 3–4 hours or until the filling is set.

Meanwhile, prepare the topping. Dip the clusters of grapes into the whisked egg white and dust with caster sugar to give a thin even coating. Leave to one side until the sugar coating has set.

Ease the sides of the tin carefully away from the cheesecake and lift the set cheesecake out on the tin base. Pipe whipped cream on top of the cheesecake and decorate with the frosted grapes.

Serves 10–12

Redcurrant cheesecake; Mocha rum cheesecake; Grape cheesecake

Mocha rum cheesecake

Metric	Imperial
100 g butter or margarine	4 oz butter or margarine
100 g caster sugar	4 oz caster sugar
225 g chocolate-coated digestive biscuits, finely crushed	8 oz chocolate-coated digestive biscuits, finely crushed

Filling:

100 g ratafias	4 oz ratafias
6 × 15 ml spoons rum	6 tablespoons rum
450 g full fat soft cheese	1 lb full fat soft cheese
4 eggs, separated	4 eggs, separated
225 g caster sugar	8 oz caster sugar
2 × 15 ml spoons instant coffee powder	2 tablespoons instant coffee powder
3 × 15 ml spoons hot water	3 tablespoons hot water
300 ml double or whipping cream	½ pint double or whipping cream
30 g powdered gelatine	1 oz powdered gelatine
5 × 15 ml spoons cold water	5 tablespoons cold water

Topping:

300 ml double or whipping cream	½ pint double or whipping cream
1 × 15 ml spoon rum	1 tablespoon rum
75 g plain chocolate, flaked	3 oz plain chocolate, flaked

Preparation time: 1 hour 35 minutes (plus chilling)

Melt the butter or margarine and sugar in a saucepan over a gentle heat and stir in the biscuit crumbs. Press evenly over the bottom of a greased loose-bottomed 25–30 cm/10–12 inch round cake tin. Chill while you make the filling.

Put a few of the ratafias to one side for the decoration. Put the remaining ratafias into a bowl and sprinkle with the rum. Cover and leave to one side. Soften the cheese in a large mixing bowl. Beat in the egg yolks, 100 g/4 oz of the caster sugar, the instant coffee dissolved in the hot water, and the cream. Put the gelatine and cold water into a small heatproof bowl over a saucepan of hot water and stir until the gelatine has dissolved. Beat the gelatine into the cheese mixture. Leave on one side until the mixture is on the point of setting.

Whisk the egg whites until stiff, then whisk in the remaining caster sugar. Fold lightly but thoroughly into the cheese mixture. Spoon half the cheese mixture into the prepared tin. Top with the rum-soaked ratafias and then add the remaining cheese mixture. Shake the tin gently to level the surface. Chill for 3–4 hours or until the filling is set.

Ease the sides of the tin carefully away from the cheesecake and lift the set cheesecake out on the tin base. For the topping, whip the double cream with the rum until thick. Pipe or swirl on top of the cheesecake. Decorate with the chocolate and reserved ratafias.

Serves 10–12

Black Forest cheesecake

Metric	Imperial
100 g butter or margarine	4 oz butter or margarine
100 g caster sugar	4 oz caster sugar
225 g chocolate-covered biscuits, finely crushed	8 oz chocolate-covered biscuits, finely crushed

Filling:

Metric	Imperial
450 g curd or sieved cottage cheese	1 lb curd or sieved cottage cheese
6 eggs, separated	6 eggs, separated
225 g caster sugar	8 oz caster sugar
60 g plain flour	2 oz plain flour
175 g plain chocolate, melted	6 oz plain chocolate, melted
3 × 15 ml spoons kirsch or brandy	3 tablespoons kirsch or brandy
300 ml soured cream	½ pint soured cream
2 × 425 g cans black cherries, drained	2 × 15 oz cans black cherries, drained

Topping:

Metric	Imperial
1 × 425 g can black cherries	1 × 15 oz can black cherries
75 g sugar	3 oz sugar
4 × 15 ml spoons black cherry jam	4 tablespoons black cherry jam
2 × 15 ml spoons brandy	2 tablespoons brandy

Preparation time: 1 hour (plus chilling)
Cooking time: 1½–1¾ hours
Oven: 160°C, 325°F, Gas Mark 3

Melt the butter or margarine and sugar in a saucepan over a gentle heat and stir in the biscuit crumbs. Press evenly over the bottom of a greased loose-bottomed 25–30 cm/10–12 inch round cake tin. Chill.
Soften the cheese in a large mixing bowl. Beat in the egg yolks, 100 g/4 oz of the sugar, the flour, melted chocolate, brandy and soured cream. Whisk the egg whites until stiff, then whisk in the remaining sugar. Fold lightly but thoroughly into the cheese mixture. Arrange the drained cherries on the biscuit base in the tin. Spoon the cheese mixture over the cherries and smooth the surface level. Bake in a preheated oven for 1½–1¾ hours or until firm but still spongy to the touch. Turn off the oven, open the door and leave the cheesecake to cool in the oven for 1 hour.
Meanwhile, prepare the topping. Drain the canned cherries and put the juice into a saucepan with the sugar and jam. Stir over a gentle heat until the sugar has dissolved, then bring to the boil and boil for 1–2 minutes. Stir in the brandy.
Ease the sides of the tin carefully away from the cheesecake and lift the cooked cheesecake out on the tin base. Brush the top and sides of the cheesecake with some of the cherry and brandy syrup. Chill for 3–4 hours. Stir the drained cherries into the remaining cherry syrup and arrange on top of the cheesecake.
Serves 10–12

Maraschino cherry cheesecake

Metric	Imperial
100 g butter or margarine	4 oz butter or margarine
100 g caster sugar	4 oz caster sugar
175 g digestive biscuits, finely crushed	6 oz digestive biscuits, finely crushed
50 g blanched almonds, chopped	2 oz blanched almonds, chopped

Filling:

Metric	Imperial
1 × 225 g jar maraschino cherries	1 × 8 oz jar maraschino cherries
450 g full fat soft cheese	1 lb full fat soft cheese
225 g caster sugar	8 oz caster sugar
4 eggs, separated	4 eggs, separated
300 ml soured cream	½ pint soured cream
30 g powdered gelatine	1 oz powdered gelatine

Topping:

Metric	Imperial
450 ml double or whipping cream, whipped	¾ pint double or whipping cream, whipped
12 maraschino cherries on stems	12 maraschino cherries on stems
75 g split almonds, toasted	3 oz split almonds, toasted

Preparation time: 1 hour 25 minutes (plus chilling)

Melt the butter or margarine and sugar in a saucepan over a gentle heat and stir in the biscuit crumbs with the chopped almonds. Press evenly over the bottom of a greased loose-bottomed 25–30 cm/10–12 inch round cake tin. Chill while you make the filling.
Drain the maraschino cherries, reserving the syrup. Roll the cherries on kitchen paper to absorb excess moisture. Soften the cheese in a large mixing bowl. Beat in 100 g/4 oz of the sugar, the egg yolks and soured cream. Put the gelatine and 8 × 15 ml spoons/8 tablespoons of the maraschino syrup (adding a little water, if necessary) into a small heatproof bowl over a saucepan of hot water and stir until the gelatine has dissolved. Beat the gelatine into the cheese mixture. Leave on one side until on the point of setting. Whisk the egg whites until stiff, then whisk in the remaining caster sugar. Fold lightly but thoroughly into the cheese mixture, together with the maraschino cherries. Spoon into the tin and chill for 3–4 hours or until set.
Ease the sides of the tin carefully away from the cheesecake and lift the set cheesecake out on the tin base. Pipe the whipped cream on top of the cheesecake and decorate with stemmed maraschino cherries and toasted almonds.
Serves 10–12

Maraschino cherry cheesecake;
Belle Hélène cheesecake; Black Forest cheesecake

Belle Hélène cheesecake

Metric	Imperial
1 thin sponge layer, 25–30 cm in diameter and 1 cm thick	1 thin sponge layer, 10–12 inches in diameter and ½ inch thick

Filling:	Filling:
2 × 425 g cans pear halves	2 × 15 oz cans pear halves
450 g full fat soft cheese	1 lb full fat soft cheese
225 g caster sugar	8 oz caster sugar
grated rind and juice of ½ lemon	grated rind and juice of ½ lemon
4 eggs, separated	4 eggs, separated
few drops of vanilla essence	few drops of vanilla essence
300 ml soured cream	½ pint soured cream
30 g powdered gelatine	1 oz powdered gelatine

Topping:	Topping:
150 ml water	¼ pint water
75 g sugar	3 oz sugar
175 g plain chocolate, broken into small pieces	6 oz plain chocolate, broken into small pieces
300 ml double or whipping cream, whipped	½ pint double or whipping cream, whipped

Preparation time: 1½ hours (plus chilling)

Press the sponge layer into a greased loose-bottomed 25–30 cm/10–12 inch round cake tin, trimming the cake to fit exactly into the bottom of the tin.
To make the filling, drain the canned pears, reserving the juice. Chop 3 of the pear halves and sprinkle over the sponge base in the tin. Keep the remaining pear halves to one side for the decoration.
Soften the cheese in a large mixing bowl. Beat in 100 g/ 4 oz of the caster sugar, the lemon rind and juice, egg yolks, vanilla essence and soured cream. Put the gelatine and 8 × 15 ml spoons/8 tablespoons of the reserved pear juice into a small heatproof bowl over a saucepan of hot water and stir until the gelatine has dissolved. Beat the gelatine into the cheese mixture. Leave on one side until on the point of setting.
Whisk the egg whites until stiff, then whisk in the remaining sugar. Fold lightly but thoroughly into the cheese mixture. Spoon the mixture into the prepared tin and shake the tin gently to level the surface. Chill for 3–4 hours or until the filling is set.
Meanwhile, for the topping, put the water and sugar into a saucepan and stir over a gentle heat until the sugar has dissolved. Bring to the boil and boil for 1–2 minutes. Add the chocolate and beat until the chocolate has completely melted. Allow to cool.
Ease the sides of the tin carefully away from the cheesecake and lift the set cheesecake out on the tin base. Pipe the top of the cheesecake with the whipped cream and arrange the reserved pear halves, rounded sides uppermost, on top. Spoon a little of the chocolate sauce over the pears and serve any remaining sauce, thinned with a little water, as an accompaniment.
Serves 10–12

Chocolate mint cheesecake

Metric
1 thin sponge layer, 25–
   30 cm in diameter and
   1 cm thick

Filling:
225 g wafer-thin chocolate
   mints
450 g full fat soft cheese
4 eggs, separated
225 g caster sugar
few drops of peppermint
   essence
300 ml double or whipping
   cream
30 g powdered gelatine
8 × 15 ml spoons water

Topping:
300 ml double or whipping
   cream
2 egg whites
75 g caster sugar

Imperial
1 thin sponge layer, 10–12
   inches in diameter and ½
   inch thick

Filling:
8 oz wafer-thin chocolate
   mints
1 lb full fat soft cheese
4 eggs, separated
8 oz caster sugar
few drops of peppermint
   essence
½ pint double or whipping
   cream
1 oz powdered gelatine
8 tablespoons water

Topping:
½ pint double or whipping
   cream
2 egg whites
3 oz caster sugar

Preparation time: 1 hour 25 minutes (plus chilling)

Press the sponge layer into a greased loose-bottomed 25–30 cm/10–12 inch round cake tin, trimming the cake to fit exactly in the bottom of the tin.

To make the filling, reserve 8–10 of the mints for decoration and chop the remainder into small pieces. Soften the cheese in a large mixing bowl. Beat in the egg yolks, 100 g/4 oz of the sugar, the peppermint essence and the cream. Put the gelatine and water into a small heatproof bowl over a saucepan of hot water and stir until the gelatine has dissolved. Beat the gelatine into the cheese mixture. Leave on one side until the mixture is on the point of setting.

Whisk the egg whites until stiff, then whisk in the remaining sugar. Fold lightly but thoroughly into the cheese mixture, together with the chopped mints. Spoon the mixture into the prepared tin and shake the tin gently to level the surface. Chill for 3–4 hours or until the filling is set.

Ease the sides of the tin carefully away from the cheesecake and lift the cheesecake out on the tin base. For the topping, whip the cream until it is quite thick. Whisk the egg whites until stiff, then whisk in the caster sugar. Fold the egg white mixture lightly into the whipped cream. Swirl the creamy meringue over the top of the cheesecake and decorate with the reserved mints, either whole or halved.

Serves 10–12

Apricot meringue cheesecake

Metric
75 g butter or margarine
3 × 15 ml spoons apricot
   jam
75 g caster sugar
225 g digestive biscuits,
   finely crushed

Filling:
450 g curd or sieved cottage
   cheese
6 eggs, separated
175 g caster sugar
60 g plain flour
6 × 15 ml spoons apricot
   jam
300 ml double or whipping
   cream

Topping:
2 egg whites
100 g caster sugar
1 × 425 g can apricot
   halves, drained

Imperial
3 oz butter or margarine
3 tablespoons apricot
   jam
3 oz caster sugar
8 oz digestive biscuits,
   finely crushed

Filling:
1 lb curd or sieved cottage
   cheese
6 eggs, separated
6 oz caster sugar
2 oz plain flour
6 tablespoons apricot
   jam
½ pint double or whipping
   cream

Topping:
2 egg whites
4 oz caster sugar
1 × 15 oz can apricot
   halves, drained

Preparation time: 50 minutes
Cooking time: 1¾ hours
Oven: 160°C, 325°F, Gas Mark 3

Melt the butter or margarine, jam and sugar in a saucepan over a gentle heat and stir in the biscuit crumbs. Press evenly over the bottom of a greased loose-bottomed 25–30 cm/10–12 inch round cake tin. Chill while you make the filling.

Soften the cheese in a large mixing bowl. Beat in the egg yolks, 75 g/3 oz of the sugar, the flour, apricot jam and cream. Whisk the egg whites until stiff, then whisk in the remaining sugar. Fold lightly but thoroughly into the cheese mixture. Spoon the mixture into the prepared tin and smooth the surface level. Bake in a preheated oven for 1¼ hours.

Meanwhile, prepare the topping. Whisk the egg whites until stiff, then whisk in 50 g/2 oz of the sugar. Fold in the remaining sugar. Top the cheesecake with the apricot halves and spread the meringue over the top. Return to the oven and continue baking for a further 25–30 minutes.

If serving the cheesecake hot, ease the sides of the tin carefully away from the cheesecake and lift the cooked cheesecake out on the tin base.

Serves 10–12

Harvey Wallbanger cheesecake

Metric
75 g butter or margarine
3 × 15 ml spoons jelly
    marmalade
75 g caster sugar
225 g digestive biscuits,
    finely crushed

Filling:
450 g full fat soft cheese
225 g caster sugar
4 eggs, separated
grated rind of 1 orange
4 × 15 ml spoons Galliano
    liqueur
300 ml double or whipping
    cream
30 g powdered gelatine
6 × 15 ml spoons orange
    juice

Topping:
300 ml double or whipping
    cream
3 × 15 ml spoons Galliano
    liqueur
2 egg whites
75 g caster sugar

Imperial
3 oz butter or margarine
3 tablespoons jelly
    marmalade
3 oz caster sugar
8 oz digestive biscuits,
    finely crushed

Filling:
1 lb full fat soft cheese
8 oz caster sugar
4 eggs, separated
grated rind of 1 orange
4 tablespoons Galliano
    liqueur
½ pint double or whipping
    cream
1 oz powdered gelatine
6 tablespoons orange
    juice

Topping:
½ pint double or whipping
    cream
3 tablespoons Galliano
    liqueur
2 egg whites
3 oz caster sugar

Preparation time: 1 hour 40 minutes (plus chilling)

Melt the butter or margarine, jelly marmalade and sugar in a saucepan over a gentle heat and stir in the biscuit crumbs. Press into a greased loose-bottomed 25–30 cm/10–12 inch round cake tin. Chill.

Soften the cheese in a large mixing bowl. Beat in 100 g/4 oz of the caster sugar, the egg yolks, orange rind, Galliano and cream. Put the gelatine and orange juice into a small heatproof bowl over a saucepan of hot water and stir until the gelatine has dissolved. Beat the gelatine into the cheese mixture. Leave on one side until the mixture is on the point of setting.

Whisk the egg whites until stiff, then whisk in the remaining sugar. Fold lightly but thoroughly into the cheese mixture. Spoon the mixture into the prepared tin and chill for 3–4 hours or until set.

Ease the sides of the tin carefully away from the cheesecake and lift the set cheesecake out on the tin base. For the topping, whip the cream with the Galliano until thick. Whisk the egg whites until stiff, then whisk in the caster sugar. Fold the meringue into the whipped cream. Pipe or swirl on top of the cheesecake. Decorate with orange segments.
Serves 10–12

Apricot meringue cheesecake; Harvey Wallbanger cheesecake; Chocolate mint cheesecake

Tropical cheesecake

Strawberry cheesecake; Tropical cheesecake;
Brandy snap cheesecake

Preparation time: 1 hour 40 minutes (plus chilling)

Metric
100 g butter or margarine
100 g caster sugar
225 g coconut biscuits,
 finely crushed

Filling:
1 × 425 g can mango pieces
450 g full fat soft cheese
225 g caster sugar
4 eggs, separated
300 ml double or whipping
 cream
40 g powdered gelatine
200 ml pineapple juice
100 g pecan nuts or
 walnuts, chopped

Topping:
50 g sugar
450 ml double or whipping
 cream, whipped
100 g desiccated coconut,
 toasted
4 kiwi fruit (Chinese
 gooseberries), peeled and
 thinly sliced
few pecans or walnuts
 (optional)

Imperial
4 oz butter or margarine
4 oz caster sugar
8 oz coconut biscuits, finely
 crushed

Filling:
1 × 15 oz can mango pieces
1 lb full fat soft cheese
8 oz caster sugar
4 eggs, separated
½ pint double or whipping
 cream
1½ oz powdered gelatine
⅓ pint pineapple juice
4 oz pecan nuts or walnuts,
 chopped

Topping:
2 oz sugar
¾ pint double or whipping
 cream, whipped
4 oz desiccated coconut,
 toasted
4 kiwi fruit (Chinese
 gooseberries), peeled and
 thinly sliced
few pecans or walnuts
 (optional)

Melt the butter or margarine and sugar in a saucepan over a gentle heat and stir in the coconut biscuit crumbs. Press evenly over the bottom of a greased loose-bottomed 25–30 cm/10–12 inch round cake tin. Chill while you make the filling.

Drain the canned mango, reserving the juice. Chop the mango pieces. Soften the cheese in a large mixing bowl. Beat in 100 g/4 oz of the sugar, the egg yolks and cream. Put the gelatine and pineapple juice into a small heatproof bowl over a saucepan of hot water and stir until the gelatine has dissolved. Beat the gelatine into the cheese mixture. Leave on one side until the mixture is on the point of setting.

Whisk the egg whites until stiff, then whisk in the remaining sugar. Fold lightly but thoroughly into the cheese mixture, together with the chopped mango and nuts. Spoon the mixture into the prepared tin and shake the tin gently to level the surface. Chill for 3–4 hours or until the filling is set.

While the cheesecake is chilling, prepare the topping: put the reserved mango juice and sugar into a saucepan and stir over a gentle heat until the sugar has dissolved. Bring to the boil and boil for 1 minute. Cool. Ease the sides of the tin carefully away from the cheesecake and lift the set cheesecake out on the tin base. Spread a thin layer of whipped cream around the side of the cheesecake and coat with the toasted coconut. Arrange the sliced kiwi fruit on top of the cheesecake and brush with the cooled mango syrup. Pipe with the remaining cream and decorate with pecans or walnuts.
Serves 10–12

Brandy snap cheesecake

Metric
*1 thin sponge layer, 25–
30 cm in diameter and
1 cm thick*

Imperial
*1 thin sponge layer, 10–12
inches in diameter and ½
inch thick*

Filling:
*24 brandy snaps
450 g full fat soft cheese
4 eggs, separated
225 g caster sugar
1 × 2.5 ml spoon ground
 ginger
generous pinch of ground
 cinnamon
300 ml double or whipping
 cream
30 g powdered gelatine
8 × 15 ml spoons water*

Filling:
*24 brandy snaps
1 lb full fat soft cheese
4 eggs, separated
8 oz caster sugar
½ teaspoon ground
 ginger
generous pinch of ground
 cinnamon
½ pint double or whipping
 cream
1 oz powdered gelatine
8 tablespoons water*

Topping:
*450 ml double or whipping
 cream, whipped
ground cinnamon or grated
 nutmeg*

Topping:
*¾ pint double or whipping
 cream, whipped
ground cinnamon or grated
 nutmeg*

Preparation time: 1½ hours (plus chilling)

Press the sponge layer into a greased loose-bottomed 25–30 cm/10–12 inch round cake tin, trimming the cake to fit exactly into the bottom of the tin.

To make the filling, coarsely crush 12–14 of the brandy snaps; reserve the remainder for the decoration. Soften the cheese in a large mixing bowl. Beat in the egg yolks, 100 g/4 oz of the sugar, the spices and cream. Put the gelatine and water into a small heatproof bowl over a saucepan of hot water and stir until the gelatine has dissolved. Beat the gelatine into the cheese mixture. Leave on one side until the mixture is on the point of setting.

Whisk the egg whites until stiff, then whisk in the remaining sugar. Fold lightly but thoroughly into the cheese mixture, together with the crushed brandy snaps. Spoon the mixture into the prepared tin and shake the tin gently to level the surface. Chill for 3–4 hours or until the filling is set.

Ease the sides of the tin carefully away from the cheesecake and lift the set cheesecake out on the tin base. Pipe some of the whipped cream on top of the cheesecake; fill the reserved whole brandy snaps with the remaining cream. Arrange the filled brandy snaps on top of the cheesecake and sprinkle the cream with a little cinnamon or nutmeg.
Serves 10–12

Strawberry cheesecake

Metric
*75 g butter or margarine
75 g caster sugar
175 g digestive biscuits,
 finely crushed*

Imperial
*3 oz butter or margarine
3 oz caster sugar
6 oz digestive biscuits,
 finely crushed*

Filling:
*450 g full fat soft cheese
4 eggs, separated
225 g caster sugar
grated rind and juice of 1
 orange
300 ml double or whipping
 cream
30 g powdered gelatine
6 × 15 ml spoons water
225 g strawberries, hulled
 and chopped*

Filling:
*1 lb full fat soft cheese
4 eggs, separated
8 oz caster sugar
grated rind and juice of 1
 orange
½ pint double or whipping
 cream
1 oz powdered gelatine
6 tablespoons water
8 oz strawberries, hulled
 and chopped*

Topping:
*300 ml double or whipping
 cream, whipped
350 g strawberries*

Topping:
*½ pint double or whipping
 cream, whipped
12 oz strawberries*

Preparation time: 1 hour 20 minutes (plus chilling)

First make the filling: soften the cheese in a large mixing bowl. Beat in the egg yolks, 100 g/4 oz of the sugar, the orange rind and juice, and the cream. Put the gelatine and water into a small heatproof bowl over a saucepan of hot water and stir until the gelatine has dissolved. Beat the gelatine into the cheese mixture. Leave on one side until the mixture is on the point of setting.

Whisk the egg whites until stiff, then whisk in the remaining caster sugar. Fold lightly but thoroughly into the cheese mixture, together with the chopped strawberries. Spoon the mixture into a greased deep 25 cm/10 inch ring mould and shake the mould gently to level the surface.

Melt the butter or margarine and sugar in a saucepan over a gentle heat and stir in the biscuit crumbs. Sprinkle evenly over the filling and press the biscuit mixture down very lightly. Chill for 3–4 hours or until the filling is set.

Ease the sides of the mould carefully away from the cheesecake and invert the set cheesecake onto a plate. Pipe with the whipped cream and fill the centre of the cheesecake ring with whole strawberries.
Serves 10–12

Chestnut cheesecake

Preparation time: 1 hour 25 minutes (plus chilling)

Metric
75 g butter or margarine
4 × 15 ml spoons honey
75 g plain chocolate,
  broken into small pieces
225 g plain semi-sweet
  biscuits, finely crushed

Imperial
3 oz butter or margarine
4 tablespoons honey
3 oz plain chocolate, broken
  into small pieces
8 oz plain semi-sweet
  biscuits, finely crushed

Filling:
450 g full fat soft cheese
1 × 425 g can unsweetened
  chestnut purée
275 g caster sugar
4 eggs, separated
few drops of vanilla essence
300 ml double or whipping
  cream
40 g powdered gelatine
8 × 15 ml spoons water
6 marrons glacé, chopped
  (optional)

Filling:
1 lb full fat soft cheese
1 × 15 oz can unsweetened
  chestnut purée
10 oz caster sugar
4 eggs, separated
few drops of vanilla essence
½ pint double or whipping
  cream
1½ oz powdered gelatine
8 tablespoons water
6 marrons glacé, chopped
  (optional)

Topping:
50 g icing sugar
2 × 15 ml spoons cocoa
  powder

Topping:
2 oz icing sugar
2 tablespoons cocoa
  powder

Melt the butter or margarine and honey in a saucepan over a gentle heat. Add the chocolate and stir until it melts. Stir in the biscuit crumbs. Press evenly over the bottom of a greased loose-bottomed 25–30 cm/10–12 inch round cake tin. Chill while you make the filling. Soften the cheese in a large mixing bowl. Beat in the chestnut purée, 175 g/6 oz of the caster sugar, the egg yolks, vanilla essence and cream. Put the gelatine and water into a small heatproof bowl over a saucepan of hot water and stir until the gelatine has dissolved. Beat the gelatine into the cheese mixture. Leave on one side until the mixture is on the point of setting.

Whisk the egg whites until stiff, then whisk in the remaining caster sugar. Fold lightly but thoroughly into the cheese mixture, together with the chopped marrons glacé, if used. Spoon the cheese mixture into the prepared tin and shake the tin gently to level the surface. Chill for 3–4 hours or until the filling is set. Ease the sides of the tin carefully away from the cheesecake and lift the set cheesecake out on the tin base. Dust the top of the cheesecake with a thin even layer of sifted icing sugar. Place a patterned paper doiley over the icing sugar and dust the sifted cocoa powder over the doiley. Carefully lift the doiley off the top of the cheesecake so as not to disturb the pattern. Serves 10–12

Rich almond cheesecake

Metric	Imperial
shortcrust pastry made with 450 g flour	shortcrust pastry made with with 1 lb flour
450 g curd or sieved cottage cheese	1 lb curd or sieved cottage cheese
6 eggs, separated	6 eggs, separated
225 g caster sugar	8 oz caster sugar
60 g plain flour	2 oz plain flour
1 × 2.5 ml spoon almond essence	½ teaspoon almond essence
3 × 15 ml spoons ground almonds	3 tablespoons ground almonds
300 ml double or whipping cream	½ pint double or whipping cream
100 g blanched almonds, chopped	4 oz blanched almonds, chopped

Topping:	Topping:
beaten egg	beaten egg
icing sugar	icing sugar
4 × 15 ml spoons raspberry jam	4 tablespoons raspberry jam

Preparation time: 50 minutes (plus chilling)
Cooking time: 1½–1¾ hours
Oven: 160°C, 325°F, Gas Mark 3

Roll out half the dough and use to line the bottom of a greased loose-bottomed 25–30 cm/10–12 inch round cake tin.
To make the filling, soften the cheese in a large mixing bowl. Beat in the egg yolks, 100 g/4 oz of the sugar, the flour, almond essence, ground almonds and cream. Whisk the egg whites until stiff, then whisk in the remaining sugar. Fold lightly but thoroughly into the cheese mixture, together with the chopped nuts. Spoon the mixture into the prepared tin.
Roll out the remaining dough and cut into thin strips, about 1 cm/½ inch wide. Arrange in a criss-cross lattice on top of the cheese filling. Brush the strips with beaten egg.
Bake in a preheated oven for 1½–1¾ hours or until firm but still spongy to the touch. Turn off the oven, open the door and leave the cheesecake there for 1 hour. Chill for 3–4 hours. Ease the sides of the tin carefully away from the cheesecake and lift out on the tin base. Dust with icing sugar and fill the squares with jam.
Serves 10–12

Rich almond cheesecake; Hazelnut cheesecake; Chestnut cheesecake

Hazelnut cheesecake

Metric	Imperial
100 g butter or margarine	4 oz butter or margarine
100 g soft brown sugar	4 oz soft brown sugar
175 g digestive biscuits, finely crushed	6 oz digestive biscuits, finely crushed
50 g ground hazelnuts	2 oz ground hazelnuts

Filling:	Filling:
100 g nut brittle	4 oz nut brittle
450 g full fat soft cheese	1 lb full fat soft cheese
225 g caster sugar	8 oz caster sugar
4 eggs, separated	4 eggs, separated
few drops of vanilla essence	few drops of vanilla essence
300 ml double or whipping cream	½ pint double or whipping cream
30 g powdered gelatine	1 oz powdered gelatine
8 × 15 ml spoons water	8 tablespoons water
75 g shelled hazelnuts, flaked	3 oz shelled hazelnuts, flaked

Topping:	Topping:
750 g shelled hazelnuts	3 oz shelled hazelnuts
100 g plain chocolate, broken into small pieces	4 oz plain chocolate, broken into small pieces

Preparation time: 1 hour 55 minutes (plus chilling)

Melt the butter or margarine and brown sugar in a saucepan over a gentle heat and stir in the biscuit crumbs with the ground hazelnuts. Press evenly over the bottom of a greased loose-bottomed 25–30 cm/10–12 inch round cake tin. Chill.
Crush the nut brittle into tiny pieces with a rolling pin. Soften the cheese in a large mixing bowl. Beat in 100 g/4 oz of the caster sugar, the egg yolks, vanilla essence and cream. Put the gelatine and water into a small heatproof bowl over a saucepan of hot water and stir until the gelatine has dissolved. Beat the gelatine into the cheese mixture. Leave on one side until the mixture is on the point of setting.
Whisk the egg whites until stiff, then whisk in the remaining caster sugar. Fold lightly but thoroughly into the cheese mixture, together with the crushed nut brittle and the flaked hazelnuts. Spoon the mixture into the prepared tin and shake the tin gently to level the surface. Chill for 3–4 hours or until set.
Meanwhile, prepare the topping. Spread out the whole hazelnuts on a freezerproof plate and freeze for 20 minutes. Melt the chocolate in a heatproof bowl over a saucepan of hot water. Stir the chilled hazelnuts into the melted chocolate so that they are evenly coated. Lift the hazelnuts out and place in small clusters on a sheet of greased greaseproof paper.
Ease the sides of the tin carefully away from the cheesecake and lift the set cheesecake out on the tin base. Decorate with clusters of chocolate-coated hazelnuts and if you like, pipe whipped cream around the edge and sprinkle with flaked hazelnuts.
Serves 10–12

79

Index